(my favorite verse)

He will cover
you with his
feathers. He
will shelter
you with his
wings. His
faithful
promises are
your armor
and
protection.

Psalm 91:4

All in All

JOURNALING DEVOTIONAL

Sophie Hudson

B&H
PUBLISHING GROUP
Nashville, Tennessee

Dedication

For my BCS girls

"I give thanks to my God for every remembrance of you."
—Philippians 1:3

Dewey Decimal Classification: 242.643
Subject Heading: DEVOTIONAL LITERATURE \ WOMEN \ CHRISTIAN LIFE

Printed in April 2017 in the United States of America.

1 2 3 4 5 6 • 21 20 19 18 17

Introduction

There's probably some perfect way to start a devotional book. There's probably some perfect combination of biblically saturated wisdom and Spirit-infused words. There's probably some perfect tone—witty but not desperate, friendly but not overly familiar—and it would no doubt work beautifully with some perfectly crafted content that's so profound it's often mistaken for poetry.

That would all be so nice.

Unfortunately, though, I am *desperately* imperfect. I say the wrong things at the wrong times. I can be more than a little goofy. And sometimes I don't know how to pronounce words, so I just say them with authority and try to act super-confident.

I'm looking at you, *quinoa.*

Here's what I have going for me, though. And don't worry. This part won't take very long.

I've spent the last twenty-ish years working with teenage girls. And about sixteen years ago, I got a job teaching English at a Christian school here in Birmingham. I've been there ever since. I don't teach English anymore; that chapter (get it?) (punny!) ended about three years ago. These days I'm more of an on-campus mama to the girls in our junior high and high school. My official title is Dean of Women, although that sounds sort of fancy considering that most days I just do a lot of listening while I hand out Kleenex and Band-Aids® and Dove® Sea Salt Caramel Dark Chocolate. But when I tell you that I adore the girls I get to serve, I mean it. They are hilarious and brilliant and thoughtful and kind. They dream big and love bigger, and life is so much better with them in it. They ask deep questions and listen with their whole hearts.

I wrote this book for them.

And I wrote it for you too. Of course I did. It just so happens that these one hundred devotions are (mostly) related to the problems and questions and heartaches and joys that have shown up in my office over the last three years. Because if I've learned anything over the span of my life—the part of my life when I've known Jesus as my Savior, in particular—it's that no matter what we're facing, He's the answer.

He really is.

(Well, I mean, I don't know that He's particularly concerned with the current state of my bangs—and oh, it is troubling—but that doesn't change the fact that for the last few mornings I've looked at my hair in the mirror and thought, *Fix it, Jesus.*)

(Sometimes we have not because we ask not, you know what I'm saying?)

And in all seriousness, my prayer is that these devotions—imperfect though they may be—will remind you of the perfect peace and perfect love and perfect grace of Jesus Christ. I pray they'll encourage you to dig deeper in your relationship with Him, to trust Him more than you did the day before, and to seek Him with your whole heart.

He is everything, you know.

No matter what. No matter where. No matter when.

He is everything.

He is our all in all.

> *He is the image of the invisible God, the firstborn of all creation.*
> *For by him all things were created, in heaven and on earth,*
> *visible and invisible, whether thrones or dominions or rulers or*
> *authorities—all things were created through him and for him.*
> *And he is before all things, and in him all things hold together.*
> *And he is the head of the body, the church. He is the beginning,*
> *the firstborn from the dead, that in everything he might be*
> *preeminent. For in him all the fullness of God was pleased to*
> *dwell, and through him to reconcile to himself all things,*
> *whether on earth or in heaven, making peace by the blood of his cross.*
> —Colossians 1:15–20 ESV

Day 1

I get it. You forget sometimes.

It stands to reason that you would. Because although, yes, this world is sacred ground—the spot you've been assigned to live and love and minister—it is also big and loud, and it often tells you it has the best solutions when it comes to you needing help. In the middle of confusion or chaos, it's not always easy to remember what's right and true.

It's even tougher when, in the middle of crisis or conflict or sadness or even some good, old-fashioned idleness, the world starts to shout:

Your help, it says, is in your reputation.
Your help, it says, is in your friend group.
Your help, it says, is in more stuff and more money.
Your help, it says, is in manipulating people to get what you want.
Your help, it says, is in working like crazy to prove your worth and your value.

But listen. *Listen.* Scripture whispers to you even while the world yells, and Scripture always tells the Truth. Scripture says, "I lift my eyes toward the mountains. Where will my help come from? My help comes from the Lord, the Maker of heaven and earth" (Psalm 121:1–2).

That's not just an answer. It's a promise. It's your safe place to rest and pray and wait.

Because the One who made this world and all that is in it—*He is your help.* No matter what, the Lord is your Source for wisdom, guidance, and direction. Through His Word, through His people, through prayer, and through the power of the Holy Spirit, He will lead you to the next right thing. He will show to you how to get out, move ahead, step aside, or get back.

And don't forget this, either: in every situation you face, He is not only your help; He is also *at work.* God never forgets, never ignores, never takes time off, never gives up, never feels caught off guard, and never stops working out His very best for you.

Sometimes situations can be so overwhelming that you don't know which way to turn. So when you're worn down and worn out and hoping the world can fix what's broken, lift up your head and look to Him instead. Remind yourself that the God of the universe is for you. Remind yourself that *He* is with you.

Remind yourself Who your helper is.

He is Father.
He is Son.
He is Holy Spirit.
He is Counselor, King, Friend, and Companion.
He is Creator, Sustainer, Redeemer, and Healer.
He is Comfort, Peace, Joy, and Hope.
He is just, forgiving, faithful, and patient.
He is constant, unchanging, merciful, and gracious.
He is all-seeing, all-knowing, all-powerful, and eternal.
He is the beginning and the end.
He is your all in all.
And He loves you completely.

Amen.

READ ACTS 17:24–28.

1. Can you think of a time you turned to something the world offers to "help" you through difficulty or pain?

_____

_____

_____

_____

2. Did that thing actually help you? Did it numb you in some way? Or did it just give you a different place to focus for a little while?

_____

_____

3. In what area(s) of your life do you need help right now? Explain.

_____

_____

4. Look at Ephesians 4:6. Write, illustrate, or doodle it here.

_____

_____

Today's Prayer

_____

_____

_____

_____

_____

_____

_____

_____

_____

_____

_____

_____

Day 2

I love college baseball. Specifically, I love Mississippi State baseball. And a few months ago, when I was walking (quickly, mind you) into the SEC Baseball Tournament so that I could watch my beloved Bulldogs play, I found myself in the middle of a mishap. The toe of my shoe caught on the edge of some concrete, and before I could say, "OH, NO—MY WEDGES HAVE BETRAYED ME," I was facedown in the concourse and experiencing some significant pain in the upper region of my right foot.

As soon as I stood up, I thought, *Well, it would seem that I've broken my foot.* And about an hour later—after I'd been X-rayed and introduced to an orthopedic boot that would be my constant companion for the next two months—a trainer confirmed that my initial diagnosis was accurate.

I spent the rest of the summer in a sassy black boot, doing my best to take care of the bone that was broken. But even though I knew, in the midst of the brokenness, that I needed to heal, there were days when I was totally annoyed by the whole healing process. It was far easier to hobble around bootless than to feel constricted by that hot, heavy boot with the straps and the Velcro and the foam. I resented the recuperation time, to be perfectly honest.

But then the Lord did the sweetest thing.

Toward the end of the aftermath of "The Unfortunate Wedge-Related Accident"—as the boot continued to protect and support what was broken—I felt the Holy Spirit remind me of three words over and over again: "Take your time." When I was tempted to hurry, when I was tempted to wear my favorite wedges, when I was tempted to think that my foot was back to normal and really, *I'm fine! The foot is good! Everything's awesome!*—that's when the Lord gave me a refrain: *Take your time.*

So often we want to hurry our healing, whether we've been physically hurt, emotionally hurt, spiritually hurt, or some combination of the three. No matter how our hurt happened, we can easily find ourselves wanting to rush the recovery. But there are three good things to remember when we find ourselves in the middle of that process:

1. What looks okay on the outside still might not be okay on the inside. *Take your time.*
2. Before you're ready to run again—whether that's literally or figuratively—you have to relearn to use what's been broken. *Take your time.*
3. Just because it doesn't hurt as much doesn't mean it's healed. *Take your time.*

Rest in the knowledge and the hope that the Lord is the Great Physician. He is our Healer. Cooperate with Him as He mends the places in you that are broken.

Thank Him for His tender loving care today.

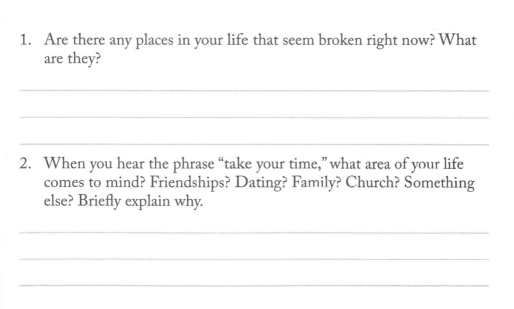

READ MATTHEW 11:27–30.

1. Are there any places in your life that seem broken right now? What are they?

_____

_____

2. When you hear the phrase "take your time," what area of your life comes to mind? Friendships? Dating? Family? Church? Something else? Briefly explain why.

_____

_____

_____

_____

3. Write out Psalm 9:10.

_____

_____

_____

_____

4. What situations are currently making you feel impatient?

_____

_____

_____

Today's Prayer

_____

_____

_____

_____

_____

_____

_____

_____

_____

_____

_____

_____

_____

Day 3

*N*ow I'm certainly no expert on spiritual warfare, but it seems to me that one of the enemy's favorite tactics—especially with women—is to come after our confidence and convince us to compare ourselves to other people. That comparison can manifest itself in all sorts of negative, one-way conversations inside our heads:

- "Sarah is so much better at talking to people than I am. I get shy and awkward when I'm around people I don't know very well, so it's no wonder I don't have many friends."
- "Everybody I know is great at something; they all seem to be gifted in one particular thing. I'm just okay at lots of things, and I'm sick of being average."
- "I would give anything to be as funny as Graham. I can't even tell a knock-knock joke without stumbling over my words."
- "If my hair looked half as good as Melanie's always does, I'd be happy every single day." (This one is not really a comparison. This one is THE ACTUAL TRUTH because my friend Melanie's hair is fantastic, and if I had her hair, I'd be happy every single day of my life.) (Also, this is not a lie from the enemy because facts are facts, people).

And in all seriousness.

There's a frequently repeated (or retweeted, as the case may be) saying that "Comparison is the thief of joy," and if you ask me, the originator of that phrase is a genius. Because comparison is the voice that screams, "You are not enough," and for some reason we not only listen to that voice, but we also *believe* it. Over and over again.

That's precisely why many of us stay trapped in a spiral of doubt and discouragement that can lead to some unmerited shame. And as soon as we think we're in the clear to jump onto steadier ground, the spiral picks us up, pulls us in, and spins us around even stronger than it did the first time.

It's a dumb way to live. And if that spiral weren't enough, there's this: comparison is a never-ending, pointless competition that no one ever wins.

You may be picking up on the fact that comparison is not my favorite.

And honestly, you have no need for comparison. The temptation to look from side to side as you size up the "competition" is not from God. It's just one of the ways the enemy likes to distract you. Don't fall for it, though. The Lord has so much more and so much better for you. He wants you to look up and reach out and walk confidently into the life He's given you.

Because you are more than enough—just as you are. There's only one person in the world with your personality, your gifts, your passions, and your abilities. You really are beyond compare.

Why settle for side-eyeing when you can get out there and get after it? Walk your road, sister.

You were made for it.

READ EPHESIANS 3:14–21.

1. In what areas of your life do you fight the temptation to compare?

_____

_____

_____

2. Has comparison ever stolen your joy? Explain your answer a little bit.

_____

_____

_____

_____

3. What are you most passionate about at this stage in your life? And if "passionate" seems like a strong word, then just list a few things that you really love to do.

_____

_____

_____

4. Write out Psalm 37:4.

_____

_____

_____

Today's Prayer

_____

_____

_____

_____

_____

_____

_____

_____

_____

_____

_____

_____

Day 4

I have a real knack for overlooking the obvious.

For example, I was every bit of twenty-eight years old when I looked at a map of the United States and suddenly realized that the western border of my home state of Mississippi was in fact the Mississippi River. It had honestly never occurred to me before.

And it was only about eight years ago that I looked at the Target sign near our house and said, "Okay—I get it now! The Target logo is an actual target!"

I don't know, y'all. I guess I just thought that the Target corporation had an affinity for dots and circles.

Given that, it probably won't be much of a shocker to learn that I was well into my thirties before I started to notice the way God reveals Himself through His creation. Suddenly the seasons started to take on much deeper meaning. (I see you, spring, and how the old stuff dies away and God replaces it with new life.) I became a certified sunset junkie—seriously couldn't get enough of them. Because here's the deal: God didn't have to make the sunsets beautiful. Same for sunrises. He could have just set an appointed time to turn the lights on and off, so to speak, and we'd have never known the difference.

But instead? He faithfully paints the sky using light and colors, clouds and shadows. The heavens are His canvas. He bookends our days with beauty, and He never creates the same painting twice.

So really, if the sky was all we had to remind us of God's majesty, that would be enough. But He gives us so much more (and these are just a few of my personal favorites):

- Bright blue oceans as deep and as vast as His love for His children
- Baby green leaves that feel like signals of hope when they first appear in the spring

- Clear, brisk lakes with water that reflects all the life that surrounds it
- Crisp, colorful autumn leaves that remind us how beautiful it can be when what's dead falls away
- Patches of sunshine on the gloomiest days because the Light *always* breaks through the darkness

If you think about it, you realize that God could have just given us some light and some water and some air and then been all, FEND FOR YOURSELVES, PEOPLE. But He's given us a garden. He's given us more beauty than our eyes can behold, and it would be such a shame if we stayed so mired down in our Snapchat stories that we missed it.

So today, if you're feeling overwhelmed, if you're feeling lonely, if you're feeling tired or hurt or sad or angry, walk outside. Look at what God has given us! Take it in with your eyes and with your heart. Ask Him to increase your awareness and your appreciation for all of His good gifts.

Soak up the beauty of this great big earth.

All creation sings His praise.

READ PSALM 19:1-6.

1. What's the most beautiful place you've ever visited?

_____

_____

2. If you had to pick, what three things in creation make you feel closest to God?

_____

_____

_____

3. Are you awed by God's gifts in nature? Or are you more of an indoors girl?

_____

_____

_____

4. Write out Psalm 19:1.

_____

_____

_____

_____

Today's Prayer

_____

_____

_____

_____

_____

_____

_____

_____

_____

_____

_____

_____

Day 5

*H*azel the Dog is the youngest member of our family. Our niece rescued her about three years ago, and as best we can tell, she had somehow gotten separated from her mother and her litter. So one Sunday afternoon, my husband and son drove to Mississippi to bring Hazel home to live with us in Alabama. I loved her as soon as I saw her. In fact, in the three years since Hazel joined our family, she and I have become so attached to each other that sometimes I worry that we're too close.

I mean, is it normal to tell your dog what you're planning to cook for supper? Or to ask your dog if your necklace looks okay with your shirt?

So Hazel and me, we're tight. But thanks to the abandonment Hazel experienced when she was a puppy, she has off-the-charts separation anxiety. If she hears me pick up my keys, she panics. If she sees us put on our shoes, she panics. And if I get home from work and don't immediately change clothes, she panics, because clearly that means I'm leaving again.

As you can imagine, Hazel panics a good bit.

A few nights ago Hazel and I were snuggling on the sofa because, well, that is what we do on most nights (please don't judge me). I was lying on my side with one arm underneath Hazel's head and the other arm draped across her tummy. I thought she was perfectly comfortable, but after a few minutes I looked at her face and realized that she was darting her eyes all around the room.

Since I like to think I can read Hazel's mind, I decided that she felt like she was trapped. So I very slowly moved the arm that was underneath her head, and I moved my other arm as well. I expected that she would jump up and run, but instead she stayed still as a stone—just as if she were still pinned in by my arms. I thought she might need some encouragement.

"Hazel," I said. "You're free, and you don't even know it!"

And then the truth of what I'd said hit me like a ton of bricks.

Because—*Yes, that could be said of so many of us!* Or maybe I should say it this way: We *know* we're free in Christ. But sometimes we sure don't live like it.

Listen. I don't know your life history. I don't know what mistakes you've made, what decisions you regret, what parts of your life you wish you'd done differently.

But here's what I do know: if you have identified with the gospel and surrendered your life to Jesus, YOU ARE FREE. If you've confessed your sin, Jesus has covered it. MOVE ON, sweet friend. I mean, I love my Hazel and all, but I'm not interested in following her example. Because it seems pretty obvious that we're not going to gain a whole lot of gospel ground with other people if we lie around acting trapped and scared when we're actually oh-so-free.

Throw off the chains. Live the life the Lord has called you to live.

He is your freedom.

Thanks be to God.

READ 2 CORINTHIANS 3:1–18.

1. How are you a little bit like Hazel? Are there areas of your life where you live as if you're not free?

_____

_____

_____

2. Do you believe you have freedom in Christ? Explain your answer.

_____

_____

_____

3. When was the last time you felt really and truly free?

_____

_____

_____

4. Write out Galatians 5:1.

_____

_____

_____

_____

Today's Prayer

_____

_____

_____

_____

_____

_____

_____

_____

_____

_____

_____

_____

_____

_____

Day 6

*Y*ou know what would be oh-so-awesome? Well, I'll tell you.

It would be oh-so-awesome if we could all make it through life without feeling hurt or left out or betrayed. It would be *fantastic* if nobody ever got her heart broken, if friends always stuck together, and if everybody left high school thinking, *Well, that just all went beautifully. I did not experience a single moment of loneliness or sadness because all I have ever known is happiness and, by the way, my hair always looked fantastic.*

However, real life and real relationships ensure that we'll experience almost all of the emotions that we tell ourselves we'd rather avoid. It occurs to me, though, that the biggest problem with pain isn't the pain itself; the biggest problem is what we do with it. Ideally we would let pain motivate us to learn and grow and work out our issues. But for lots of us, I think, hurt and pain are things we tuck away and push down and block out. We know that we're not okay, but we decide it's easier to pretend than to be vulnerable and open up about what's really going on.

And all too often, we cope by trying to push the pain out of the way. We don't deal with how we actually feel about our parents' divorce or a grandparent's difficult diagnosis or that person who seems to specialize in making pointed, sarcastic remarks that sting our hearts. And when we don't deal with the pain, we sometimes try to treat our emotional wounds with what amounts to some spectacularly superficial treatment. We just ignore the hurt that's piled up beneath the surface, and then we wonder why we don't feel close to anyone.

We blame people, but pain is the problem.

Pain becomes baggage that we carry from friendship to friendship, all the while hoping that if we just assign different, better-sounding words to what we're carrying—or if we just camouflage it—life will magically be better.

So here's a hot tip, and you don't even have to pay me for it: *That pain isn't going anywhere until you let Jesus have His way with it.*

Remember this: Jesus knows pain. He knows sorrow. He knows betrayal. He knows fear. He experienced all of the above (and so much more) during His thirty-three years on this earth.

And maybe today is the day that you hand a piece of that pain over to Him. It doesn't have to be a big, dramatic deal. Just say something like this:

Lord, I'm tired of pretending. I know this (whatever it is) is hurting me more than it's helping me. I know I'm trying to hide it and keep it in the dark. But today I'm placing it in the Light. I'm handing it to You. I know that You're a safe place to be vulnerable and to be real. Ultimately, no healing happens without You. So I pray for wisdom, I pray for peace, and I pray for Christian friends and mentors to stand beside me. In Jesus' name.

Trust me. That pain is too much to carry alone.
Lay it down.

READ PSALM 69:1-17.

1. What is currently causing you pain? Be specific, and take as much time and space to write as you need.

_____

_____

_____

2. Have you told anyone about anything you listed in #1?

_____

_____

_____

_____

3. What do you want to ask God about your pain? What do you need to tell Him?

_____

_____

_____

4. Write out Psalm 119:76.

_____

_____

_____

_____

Today's Prayer

_____

_____

_____

_____

_____

_____

_____

_____

_____

_____

_____

_____

Day 1

When we were writing our first books, my friend Melanie and I began sending each other chapters as we finished them. Even though sometimes it felt like the most vulnerable thing in the world to let another set of eyes look at a chapter I'd written, the accountability and feedback were invaluable.

About a year ago, when I was working on my previous book, I was walking to my office when a thought came to me out of nowhere. It hit me so hard that I went straight to the computer and typed it out, and I remember thinking how it was a weird sentence for me to write because it's not how I normally talk or even think. I put it in the chapter, and I was immediately uncomfortable with how people might respond to it. So, I quickly wrote a joke underneath it—a joke that made light of the idea and diminished its impact.

Then I finished the chapter and sent it to Melanie. And maybe winced a little bit.

The next day Melanie sent me her feedback, and it was all very kind and encouraging. Then she hit me with some truth; she told me that the joke I'd written took away from the sentence before it. She said, "Own that God gave you that insight and that you wrote it."

So I took out the joke. It didn't just change the tone of the chapter; it changed the tone of the book. Melanie's words gave me the confidence I needed to write what I was supposed to write.

And after the book came out, that sentence was the one people mentioned to me more than any other.

So often, I think, when we love to do something like writing or singing or running or whatever that "thing" happens to be, our temptation is to hold it close to our chest with our arms wrapped ALL THE WAY AROUND IT. We don't let anybody else peek in for fear that they'll laugh or judge or criticize us. We start to tell ourselves that our interests are dumb and we're not any good and really there are thousands of people who can do that thing we love to do.

And we're right, you know. There are thousands of people who can do whatever it is we love to do. What we forget is that we *need* thousands of people. After all, wouldn't the world be so boring if we only had, like, seven chefs?

But my bigger point is this: if there's something you love to do—maybe even something you feel like you were made to do—then look for a friend (or friends!) who will cheer you on and tell you the truth. Make yourself vulnerable and share your talent with them. If they're people who really love you and truly have your best interest at heart, they'll be honest with you. They'll spur you on. They'll push you in the right direction—even if the direction isn't what you expected. They may even help you discover a talent you didn't know you had.

That thing you love to do might not feel as safe. You might not be able to hold it quite as close. But it'll be better—and you'll be braver—for sharing it.

Own it, sister. God has big plans for you.

READ 1 PETER 4:7–11.

1. What's a gift (or gifts) that you know the Lord has given you? Remember that His gifts come in many forms.

_____

_____

_____

2. Do you tend to downplay your gifts, or do you use them confidently?

_____

_____

_____

3. Who consistently encourages you? Who has become a safe place to share your ideas and dreams?

_____

_____

_____

4. Write out 2 Corinthians 4:7.

_____

_____

_____

_____

Today's Prayer

_____

_____

_____

_____

_____

_____

_____

_____

_____

_____

_____

_____

_____

_____

Day 8

This morning I was fixing a late breakfast for my family, and it dawned on me in the middle of it all that maybe we should pay more attention to biscuits.

Seriously. And not just because of their fluffy, buttery, high-carb goodness. Those qualities are admirable, certainly, but biscuits actually teach a way bigger lesson, one that I didn't learn until a few years ago.

So first, a little history.

As a Southern girl, I grew up watching my grandmother make biscuits. I never paid much attention to the finer points of the process because she made it look effortless. But when I got older and started to make biscuits myself, I was always frustrated by how flat and dense mine seemed in comparison. In fact, I was such a biscuit-making failure that I eventually stopped trying altogether.

One day, though, I decided to investigate where I was going wrong, and I picked up on a tiny detail that I'd either ignored or forgotten in all my previous attempts: *when you put biscuits on a baking sheet, the sides should touch slightly.*

So I tried it. And y'all, it transformed my whole biscuit-making experience. Suddenly the biscuits I was taking out of the oven had height like the ones Mamaw Davis used to make, and all it took was a little side-by-side contact.

If you think about it, that'll preach.

Because if we want to grow in our faith—in wisdom and stature and favor with God and man (Luke 2:52)—then we need to be shoulder-to-shoulder with other people. It's a counter-cultural concept for sure. We hear way more these days about people wanting their space and trying to carve out some alone time. But when we're talking about truly "rising up" (get it? I am here for all your pun needs) in our relationships with the Lord and with each other, then we have to be close enough to touch. Granted, we don't need to pile on each other or smother each other—that would be counter-productive—but we also don't need to be so far apart that we're isolated or separated from other believers.

What does that look like in a practical, real-life sense? Well, maybe it means you join a small group at church. Maybe you get involved in a Bible study. Maybe you and a couple of friends link arms and decide to mentor some younger girls at your school. Maybe you ask some older girls to meet with you once a week to read the Bible and pray. Maybe you talk to your parents about starting a family devotion time a couple of nights a week.

The recipe doesn't have to be exactly the same, but that part about "slightly touching"? It is key. And if you're tempted to think otherwise, just look at Scripture: Jesus had His disciples. Paul had Timothy. Mary had Elizabeth. Naomi had Ruth. David had Jonathan. They all loved God and trusted Him completely. And their "slightly touching," shoulder-to-shoulder fellowship equipped and enabled each of them to support each other, trust God's plans, and live obediently.

The biscuits know what's up, y'all.

READ HEBREWS 10:19-25.

1. If you could choose two people in your life with whom you'd stand shoulder-to-shoulder, who would they be? Why?

_____

_____

_____

2. Is there anyone in your life who is "shoulder-to-shoulder"? Anyone who has an up-close view of what's going on? Who is it?

_____

_____

_____

3. Why do you think isolation is so easy?

_____

_____

_____

4. Write out Romans 1:11–12.

_____

_____

_____

_____

Today's Prayer

_____

_____

_____

_____

_____

_____

_____

_____

_____

_____

_____

_____

Day 9

I hope you don't find this hard to believe, but since I work with teenage girls every day, I sometimes have to deal with a little bit of drama.

Shocking, I know.

Sometimes the drama is because of a misunderstanding. Sometimes it's because of a social media post (if I could, I would insert all the red-faced emojis right here). Sometimes it's because of a boy.

More often than not, the drama is directly tied to words. And believe me, there are all sorts of word-related offenders: a hastily sent email, a group text gone wrong, a sarcastic remark in the hallway, a rumor that's passed along thoughtlessly—we could go on and on.

If you've ever been on the receiving end of one of those things, you know how much it can hurt. But sometimes, we're the ones who do the hurting, and I understand why it happens. We're always looking for ways to feel connected to other people—to feel accepted and "safe"—so when the enemy dangles bait that gives us a chance to be a mocker as opposed to mocked, to be the scorner instead of scorned, we can feel tempted to lunge at that seemingly tasty morsel. So we start a rumor, share some gossip, roast the new girl—and we act like it's all in good fun.

After all, the bait looks delicious, right?

But don't be fooled, sweet girls: that bait is a trap. And that trap will hook you and hold you for longer than you ever intended to stay there.

That's why it's critical to use our words well. Proverbs 18:21 tells us that, "Death and life are in the power of the tongue, and those who love it will eat its fruits" (ESV). So every time we speak, we are choosing life or death.

Let me repeat that.

Every time we speak, we are choosing life or death.

We can build up, encourage, love, and support. Or we can tear down, wound, hate, and reject.

So, I just want to offer three quick suggestions that will hopefully remind us of how important it is to speak life today:

1. **Every single person is made in the image of God. Every. Single. One.** It's good to remember that before we share the latest rumor or pass along "news" that's really none of our business. The person you're tempted to talk about is precious in God's sight. Choose your words carefully.
2. **Empathy changes how we respond.** Instead of firing off a sarcastic remark, take ten seconds to really think about how the other person feels—and how you feel when people are unkind to you. Think about the possibility that what you and the other person really need is a conversation, not an argument.
3. **It's so much more rewarding to create a culture of honor** and esteem than it is to settle for a culture of mean. And if you're tempted to think the culture can't be any different—that you can't make a difference—then stand up for someone who's having a tough time. You'll see what an impact even one person can have.

Give grace. Speak life. Your words are more powerful than you know.

READ EPHESIANS 4:25–32.

1. Have you ever been mean to another person because you wanted to fit in with a group? Did you learn any lessons as a result?

_____

_____

2. Have you ever been wounded by another person's words? Don't write the words down—we don't want to give them any power—but think about and write about what it took to recover from that particular hurt.

_____

_____

3. Can you remember a time when someone's encouragement meant the world to you? What did that person say to you?

_____

_____

4. Write out Proverbs 12:18.

_____

_____

_____

_____

Today's Prayer

_____

_____

_____

_____

_____

_____

_____

_____

_____

_____

_____

_____

_____

Day 10

At some point in your life, you're going to make choices that seem weird to other people. It might be that you start a non-profit while you're still in high school, or you delay starting college so you can spend a few years serving refugees overseas, or you walk away from a lucrative career so that you can go to culinary school. The *when* really isn't the important part. The important part is that you will tell people about your "weird" decision, and regardless of their reactions you will stand firm and be courageous enough to follow through with what you know is the right choice.

Because underneath all the seemingly weird, you know beyond a shadow of a doubt that it's where the Lord has led you.

Take David and Goliath, for instance.

For starters, David initially went to the Israelites' army camp on an errand for his father. He was supposed to take a few items to his brothers and then deliver some cheese.

Hi. I'm the unlikely future king of Israel. Can I interest you in some cheese?

(I know that's not really what happened.)

(But for some reason it delights me.)

(And it's also a great reminder that God sometimes places life-changing events in the middle of the most mundane chores.)

But after David got to camp (with the cheese!), Goliath challenged the Israelites, and David declared that he'd fight the giant and defend Israel (weird decision #1). Saul tried to talk David out of battling the giant, but David made a passionate case that he was the man for the job. Eventually Saul relented and proceeded with the natural next step: he clothed David with his armor. After all, David had served as Saul's armor bearer, so David actually *wearing* that armor probably seemed like a pretty logical progression.

There was only one problem.

David didn't want to wear Saul's helmet or breastplate. He didn't want to carry his sword. In fact, he went to Saul and said, "I can't walk in these. . . . I'm not used to them" (1 Samuel 17:39). And he took them off (weird decision #2).

In the end David went with what he knew: a staff, five smooth stones, and a slingshot (if you're keeping score at home, that's weird decision #3). It wasn't the most sophisticated line of defense, but David knew that it was exactly how he needed to face his foe. He knew it would give him the best shot at defeating Goliath.

Our big takeaway? Contrary to what we tell ourselves, we don't all have to "suit up" the same. Decisions that seem weird to others are A-OK when they come with the Lord's covering. The Holy Spirit leads us individually. We need to be so careful that we don't fall into the trap of feeling like serving God requires following somebody else's formula, you know?

Because at the end of the day, weird is relative, but obedience is essential.

So talk to God. And listen. He'll let you know if your weird is just weird or just right.

READ 1 SAMUEL 17:41-50.

1. Can you think of a decision you've made that, at first glance, might seem strange to others? Explain.

_____

_____

2. What are the benefits to "resting in the weird," so to speak? What's the upside of obedience—even if other people don't understand?

_____

_____

3. Do you ever feel pressured to "go along to get along"? Why is it sometimes so difficult to go against the grain?

_____

_____

_____

4. Write out Isaiah 30:21.

_____

_____

_____

_____

Today's Prayer

_____

_____

_____

_____

_____

_____

_____

_____

_____

_____

_____

Day 11

This past Sunday was sort of a yuck day in our house. A big misunderstanding was in the works before I'd even started to drink my first cup of coffee, and our family had barely started to address the issue when everything ramped up to a full-fledged disagreement. By that point, our "spirited fellowship" had kept us from making it to church, I had cried so much that there was no point in wearing eye make-up, and at least two of us were wondering if there was any way to salvage the day.

Here's what I wanted to do: stay in my pajamas forever.

Here's what we did: met two families from our small group for lunch. Even though we didn't necessarily feel like it. And it turned out to be such a good decision.

Here's why:

As we sat around the table and shared chips and salsa and cheese dip and conversation, my family began talking about how our morning had taken a nosedive. And as we shared a few of the details that were *starting* to become funny (but only in the sense of *Oh sweet mercy—remember when we nearly lost our minds over this about three hours ago?*), our friends listened with zero judgment and condemnation. Instead, they said things like, "Hey, we've been there" and "We understand. It happens to everybody."

They jumped in with support and affirmation, and as a result of that, they removed our initial embarrassment about, you know, MISSING CHURCH BECAUSE WE WERE ARGUING.

I've thought a lot about what happened that Sunday, not because I want to venture into family counseling (oh, heavens no), but because the Lord taught me a good lesson about moving forward after conflict—no matter what our stage of life might be.

It's so easy—and probably pretty common—to take those less-than-perfect moments from family life and try to hide them out of sight. But whether it's an argument with someone we love, a moment when we've been caught acting less than our best, a gigantor misunderstanding with a sibling, or a time when we've felt a little bit betrayed, we really can bounce back. We can be better. And we'll do well, I think, to remember three things.

1. **Everyone is broken (Romans 3:23).** We all make mistakes. We all experience the occasional relational train wreck. But the Lord, in His kindness, mends hearts, soothes hurt feelings, and puts us back together again.
2. **Move through it and not around it (Psalm 23:4).** Speak the truth in love. Have a hard conversation if necessary and settle it—whatever "it" is. Unresolved conflict leads to disproportionate drama. Drama is a drag. And also exhausting.
3. **Rest in the Lord's steadfast love (Psalm 31:7).** He knows when you feel embarrassed or ashamed. Let Him comfort you through Scripture, through prayer, through worship, and through His people. He is so faithful.

It might make you smile to know that even though we missed church Sunday morning, we made it to the Sunday night service. And as we sat down in our normal row, I thought, *Well, this feels like grace.*

Second chances always do.

READ LAMENTATIONS 3:22–24.

1. Has there ever been a time you opened up to someone about a family conflict and were met with grace? Or have you extended that grace to someone else? What did you learn from that experience?

2. Have you ever thought about how God comforts us through people? Who has been a comfort to you lately? How so?

_____

_____

3. Look up a song by Andrew Peterson called "I Want to Say I'm Sorry." Listen to it and write down any lyrics that stand out to you.

_____

_____

4. Why does unforgiveness take such a toll in families?

_____

_____

_____

Today's Prayer

_____

_____

_____

_____

_____

_____

_____

_____

_____

_____

_____

Day 12

*L*et's talk about church. I'll start.

I grew up in church. Our family was there every single Sunday morning and Sunday night unless we were out of town or someone was sick. And you'd better have been, like, throw-up sick. Otherwise you could plan on running a fever or managing your cold while sitting front and center in Sunday School.

So what I'm saying is that church was a big priority.

When I went to college, though, I bailed on church the first chance I had. There was no one to make me get up and get dressed and get myself to the church house, so I opted out. Typically, I would sleep in before I'd make a late-morning run to Popeye's for some fried chicken. (Even though I couldn't be bothered with church, I never lost my affection for Sunday lunch.) And if you had asked me, I would have told you that God and I were good, but I didn't see much need for church—because really, I just didn't get that much out of it.

We don't have room enough or time enough for me to tell you all the ways that my "freedom" from church eventually held me captive. It was a bad, shortsighted decision—one of my all-time worst, to be honest. So now, when I talk to girls who are about to go to college (which, in my opinion, is the most fun time of your whole life), my very first piece of advice is this:

Join a church.

Don't just find a church. Don't just visit a lot of churches. Join a church. Put down roots in a local congregation. Make a commitment. It's so important. Here's why:

1. **You need a place to transition.** It's tougher to live out your faith when you're away from the safety of home. And I hate to break it to you, but consistently spending time with God isn't necessarily the top trait of new college students. A local church gives you a safe place to ask questions and mature in your faith. This is critical.

2. **You need to keep growing.** I still loved the Lord even when I wasn't in church. But I stopped growing as a believer because I wasn't being taught from the Word on a regular basis, and really, there wasn't any element of worship in my life. Sitting under the authority and teaching of a loving pastor—especially one who knows you personally—is a gift that keeps on giving. Don't miss it.

3. **You need the community.** Members of a local church will care for you and look out for you. They will strengthen you and challenge you and hold you accountable. They will comfort you when you hurt and love you just because. You will be stronger and wiser for the time you spend with other Christians. Let them take care of you.

As a believer you're part of the family of Christ no matter where you go. The local church is your home base for fellowship and discipleship and service. Thanks be to God.

READ EPHESIANS 4:11–16.

1. What are some of your childhood memories from church? Or, if you haven't grown up in church, do you feel as if you missed out on anything? Explain.

_____

_____

_____

2. Think about your favorite pastors or Bible study leaders. How has their teaching encouraged you?

_____

_____

3. Has the Lord ever used a sermon to change you? Reflect on that and write out as many examples as come to mind.

_____

_____

_____

4. If you're not part of a local church, list three or four you'd like to visit. And if you are part of a local church, list three or four things you love and appreciate about your church.

_____

_____

_____

Today's Prayer

_____

_____

_____

_____

_____

_____

_____

_____

_____

_____

_____

Day 13

Y'all have probably never done this, so feel free to just sit back and think about how awesomely mature you are while I make a small confession:

Sometimes I get really worried about what's down the road.

And I'm not speaking literally, of course. I don't live in fear of the drugstore near the entrance to our neighborhood. I'm talking about the *figurative* road—what the future holds. And I don't even confine my worry to a specific area; I much prefer to worry about all the things. So on any given day that might mean I worry about my family, my friends, our dog, a conversation I need to have, a football game, my job, a doctor's appointment, whatever. You name it, and I have probably worried about it. Because I don't mean to brag, but I am an *excellent* worrier.

Try not to be jealous, everybody.

Not too long ago I was talking to some high school seniors, and they started listing everything that scares them about college. Somehow that list transitioned into their worries about relationships and marriage and children and careers, and before you know it they were having a big ole festival-o'-fear.

I think I can speak for the group and say that it wasn't even a little bit of fun.

And you know why it wasn't fun (besides the fact that the whole conversation was a bummer, of course)? Worry isn't God's best for us. On some level it's a declaration that we don't trust Him, we don't believe He goes before us, and we don't think His plan is good enough. We don't necessarily *intend* for that to be the outcome when we get bogged down in all the what-ifs related to, say, a conflict we wish we'd handled better. But ultimately our concern is that God won't be able to get us through whatever situation He has in store for us.

That is crazy talk, y'all.

A few weeks ago our pastor preached a sermon on worry and anxiety. Toward the end, as he encouraged us to surrender and rest in the peace of God, he said something that was positively profound to me: *Stay out of the future.*

Stay. Out. Of. The. Future.

Isn't that so good? Because there is something about worry (and the accompanying anxiety) that turns all of us into some really jacked-up fortune tellers. It's a strange thing, our worst-case-scenario "certainty" that is solely the product of our imagination.

So, today let's remind ourselves to *stay out of the future.* There's no good reason to rob ourselves of the peace we have in Jesus. Here and now—in this present day, in these present circumstances—is where we're supposed to be. We can trust Him with what's next because He loves us, He is for us, and He is faithful.

He is our all in all.

READ MATTHEW 6:25–34.

1. On a scale of 1 to 5, how big of an issue is worry for you?

_____

_____

_____

_____

2. What do you think you are trying to control when you worry? Explain.

_____

_____

_____

_____

3. Was there a time when you were super worried about something—and then that something didn't even happen? What was that experience like?

_____

_____

_____

4. Write out, doodle, illustrate Matthew 6:34.

_____

_____

_____

Today's Prayer

_____

_____

_____

_____

_____

_____

_____

_____

_____

_____

_____

_____

_____

_____

Day 14

This past summer was not my favorite. I hope it's okay to say that. I certainly don't want to hurt summer's feelings. But from start to finish, it was sort of an overachiever with the hard stuff. First, I broke my foot (I believe we've discussed that), and then there was a certain situation that was causing me a considerable amount of emotional distress (vague, I know, but it's the best I can do), and then, at the end of June, my mama died.

Oh, my mama. Y'all. I'm still not ready to write about that. We'll talk about her later though. Promise.

But when she died? Well, go ahead and prepare yourself for an understatement: *I was really sad.*

If you had asked me in mid-May, I would have told you that summer was going to be *so awesome*! And there was going to be *big fun*! And we were going to make *the best memories*! Instead, though, summer came in like an angry tide. It was one wave of heartache after another.

And it's just a guess, but you've probably had times in your life that felt the same way. Maybe it was a parent losing a job followed by a broken friendship. Maybe it was difficulty in school followed by a challenging sports season. Maybe it was a frustrating health issue followed by constant conflict with your boyfriend.

So when one angry tide after another keeps knocking you over, what do you do?

Here's what: you hold on to Jesus, and you get back up again.

YES, MA'AM.

After all, we need not forget that in the middle of our hardships, we still have victory in Christ (Romans 8:38–39). John 16:33 says this: "I have told you these things so that in me you may have peace. You will have suffering in this world. Be courageous! I have conquered the world."

We have hope even when life gets hard.

If there's a biblical poster child for tough times, it's Job. He lost his money, his possessions, his family, his friends, and his health. (Honestly,

Job's life makes my summer look like a vacation.) But even in the middle of his pain, Job didn't give up and he didn't lose faith. He knew Who held his victory. In Job 19:25 he said, "For I know that my Redeemer lives, and at the last he will stand upon the earth" (ESV).

Isn't that good news? WE HAVE A REDEEMER. And when we go through trials, He continues to shower us with grace upon grace: His peace, His comfort, His people, His Word. In the Lord we can find peace even when we don't love our circumstances. We may lose a few battles along the way, but *He has won the war.*

You are a daughter of the Most High King. You are a warrior. You are more than a conqueror (Romans 8:37). That angry tide has nothing on who you are in Him. Grab hold of your Savior, and get up again.

You can do it.

READ 2 CORINTHIANS 4:8-12.

1. What's the angry tide in your life right now? What's threatening to knock you down?

_____

_____

_____

2. Has there ever been a time in your life when you felt defeated? What did the Lord teach you through that?

_____

_____

_____

3. Do you have friends or family members who are in an especially difficult season right now? Make a list, and at some point in the next week, write them notes of encouragement. The Lord will use your words to comfort them and remind them of His love.

4. What verses remind you of the strength you have in Jesus? Write them out here.

Today's Prayer

Day 15

*I*f you have grown up in the church or if you have participated for even a short while in a youth group, then you have probably—at least once—heard a lesson or a sermon about sexual purity. I don't know if you've noticed, but it's kind of a hot topic.

Maybe I shouldn't have used the word *hot*. Maybe that has a lustful connotation. I don't even know.

But seriously, we're all familiar with the Sexual Purity Moment (can I trademark that?), and it's oh-so-important. But before we talk about that, let's talk about something that is less frequently discussed but nonetheless oh-so-important. Ready?

Absolutely enjoy your friendships with guys, but be aware that sometimes the emotional boundaries can get a little tricky.

Perhaps I should explain.

There is a certain comfort that comes from having guy friends. I for one am forever grateful for my guy friends from high school and college. You can laugh together, hang out together, and enjoy the sweetest brother-sister-type relationships. But sometimes those guy-girl friendships can get mired down in what I like to refer to as Significant Relational Weirdness.

(I'll go ahead and trademark SRW along with the Sexual Purity Moment. Just FYI.)

The deal with the SRW guys is that it typically happens when you're super close to someone of the opposite sex. Maybe you text for hours every night. Maybe you analyze your deep feelings. You carry each other's secrets. You discuss your relationships with the Lord and the areas where you struggle. It's not that your relationship is physical, but there's an emotional familiarity that is pretty deep and vulnerable.

Don't get me wrong: guy-girl friendships are awesome. But occasionally the awesome can get confusing. Maybe that's because your feelings go beyond "just friends." Maybe that's because his do. And before you realize it, you've given away some significant pieces of your heart to someone who may not understand—or want—the responsibility of honoring your heart, soul, and mind.

So what's the answer? To stop being friends with boys and completely eliminate the possibility of SRW from your life?

Of course not.

But relationships follow a progression. And if we know that Scripture admonishes us to "guard your heart above all else, for it is the source of life" (Proverbs 4:23), then we have to ask the Lord to help us keep a check on its intake so that its output is healthy and pure and good. Pray about your relationships with your guy friends. Ask the Lord to give wisdom to both of you, to help you keep a check on when your emotional involvement has progressed to something more than "just friends." And if that happens? It's not a bad thing at all, but if those feelings aren't mutual, you may develop expectations that frustrate or confuse the other person. Ask your parents and trusted friends to pray for you, to keep an eye on you, and to speak the truth in love when your heart's intake or output seems "off" in relation to that friendship.

The way to maintain healthy boundaries isn't just to make up your mind to be healthy. It's to surrender your heart first to the Lord, to pray with sincerity for God's best for your heart and mind, to enlist trusted Christian friends to encourage and love you—and then pray you'll *listen* to the Lord and His people.

Friendship is such a gift. So is the ability to be wise and take care of each other.

READ ROMANS 12:9–21.

1. What do you enjoy about having guy friends?

_____

_____

_____

2. Has SRW ever infiltrated those friendships? If so, what did the Lord teach you through that experience?

_____

_____

3. Do you ever look to your friendships for a sense of validation or approval? How can that be an issue in your spiritual life?

_____

_____

4. Read Deuteronomy 6:5, and write it out here.

_____

_____

Today's Prayer

_____

_____

_____

_____

_____

_____

_____

_____

_____

_____

_____

_____

Day 16

*T*here are no doubt hundreds of cultural factors we could blame—not to mention the fact that we have a bent toward brokenness—but the number of young women who are struggling with the pressure to be perfect is at an all-time high.

Granted, I'm no statistician. But I work with high school girls. I talk to lots of college girls. And the running list of unreasonable expectations that girls are putting on themselves?

It's exhausting, y'all. Somehow we've allowed society to set an impossible standard, and countless young women evaluate and define themselves by how well they think they measure up.

As a general rule, we just don't give ourselves—or each other—a whole lot of grace.

Somewhere along the way too many girls have bought into the belief that they have to be the best at everything. But that's a lie. You can absolutely live a life that honors God without being an academic stand-out or an extracurricular all-star. There's no list of boxes you have to perfectly check off to impact others for the cause of Christ.

And you certainly don't have to navigate the sometimes rocky terrain of your teens and twenties without messing up, embarrassing yourself, or failing in spectacular fashion.

No one is handing out any prizes for perfect, my friend. Only Jesus earns that prize.

One day last week I heard a story about a college student who recently faced an unpleasant consequence. The mistake she made wasn't life-altering, necessarily, but it resulted in some uncomfortable conversations as she sought forgiveness and restoration in a relationship she'd damaged. Afterward the girl's mom told her how proud she was of her and encouraged her to put the incident behind her and move on, but before her mom could finish her pep talk, the daughter interrupted her.

"I'm just so mad at myself. So *frustrated* with myself. I KNOW BETTER. I should have never done what I did! How could I have made that mistake when I knew it was the wrong thing to do?"

Immediately the mom recognized that her daughter's true frustration was that she'd behaved in a way that was less than perfect (and for the record, we're all less than perfect, but we forget that sometimes). So when her daughter finished talking, the mom said this:

"Hey, you don't have to be perfect. Just be teachable."

"Ma'am?" the daughter replied.

"You're human. You make mistakes. You're not going to get it right all the time. But when you mess up, pray that you'll learn what the Lord is teaching you. It's so much more rewarding than trying to be perfect."

And it is.

Ultimately striving for perfection (or pretending to be perfect) is a way we try to earn our own salvation and takes away our need for Christ. But being teachable keeps God's standard right where it should be—above everything else—so that in our humility and surrender, He gets the glory.

You don't have to be perfect. (Jesus did that for you!) Just be teachable. Grace is waiting on you there.

READ ROMANS 8:1-11.

1. Have you ever wrestled with perfectionism? How did that play out in your life? Was it a struggle in terms of your appearance, your achievements, your reputation? Talk about that a little bit.

2. Have you ever pretended to be perfect in a certain area (this is my story, by the way) because you feared the criticism or judgment of other people if you were completely honest? Explain.

3. What are some areas of your life where you need to be teachable?

4. Read Romans 11:6, and write it out here.

Today's Prayer

Day 17

When I was fourteen, I went to a beach retreat with my youth group. We stayed across the street from the Gulf at a "conference center" that was essentially cement block barracks, and I thought we were all so grown up to be away from home and on the beach, and clearly ninth-grade life was just way more glamorous than I ever dreamed it would be.

Bless my heart.

Early on in the retreat, I decided that there were two things I wanted to take home with me: (1) a closer relationship with the Lord and (2) a tropical tan. The fact that I do not have the genetic make-up (blonde hair, blue eyes, fair skin) for a tropical tan was really of no concern to me. I told myself that if I just spent enough time in the sun, I'd be beautifully bronzed by the end of our trip.

Now obviously there's nothing wrong with wanting to go outside and soak up a little bit of sun, but my strategy was way off. I skipped putting on sunscreen because I thought it would slow down the tanning process. I spent several hours sitting next to the water without the aid of sunscreen or any sort of hat. It was pretty much just some dangerous UV rays and me.

Suffice it to say that within an hour of getting in the van to go home, I was sick as a dog—the sickest I have ever been in my life. And sun poisoning wasn't my only souvenir from our time at the beach. Because within a couple of days, water blisters covered my chest and shoulders.

You might say that the sun sent me home with more than I was bargaining for. And somewhere within all that sun-scorched drama of my own making, there's a pretty good lesson.

So often there's something that we really want—something that's a perfectly fine and good and worthwhile goal (maybe not, you know, *a tan*, but still)—but the way we go about achieving what we're after isn't even a little bit wise.

That whole wisdom thing? It's critical. Because if we've ever tried to get healthy by starving ourselves, or attempted to win an election by spreading a rumor about an opponent, or shown up for an audition without taking time to prepare, we know how tempting it can be to do lots of perfectly permissible things the wrong way. That's why we can't underestimate our deep need for wisdom. No matter what goals are in front of us, we want to walk toward them in a way that honors the Lord and remains mindful of His very best for us.

Proverbs 4:7 says, "Wisdom is supreme—so get wisdom. And whatever else you get, get understanding." Before we move ahead with any of our manmade plans, our first step should be to seek wisdom. Pray. Look to Scripture. Seek the counsel of people you trust. We don't just want to be smart by human standards (and certainly I was missing even that component during my Unfortunate Tanning Experiment); we want to be wise by God's standards. That requires humility, surrender, and insight that can only come from Him.

Be wise.

(P.S. And wear sunscreen.)

READ JAMES 1:2-8.

1. Think back over the last few years. Can you think of a situation where your intentions were good but your approach or strategy was lacking in wisdom?

_____

_____

2. So often we associate wisdom with older people. How is it possible for younger people to be wise even though they don't have as much life experience?

_____

_____

3. The Lord enriches our lives with the gift of wise people. Who are the people in your life who are genuinely wise—people who know how to handle almost any situation in a way that's consistent with Scripture?

_____

_____

4. Look up Proverbs 1:7. Write, doodle, or illustrate it here.

_____

_____

_____

Today's Prayer

_____

_____

_____

_____

_____

_____

_____

_____

_____

_____

_____

_____

_____

Day 18

So everybody gets *needs* and *wants* confused from time to time, right?

And more than likely all of us have had a moment when we thought this car or that sweater or this pair of running shoes—things that we've told ourselves we need—will somehow transform the quality of our lives and fix all our problems.

When I was a junior in college, the thing that was going to change my life in a thousand ways was a Dooney & Bourke purse. I could picture myself walking to class with "my Dooney" (as I called it) on my shoulder, and I could imagine what it would feel like to open the Dooney and take out my wallet to buy my lunch at Popeye's.

Because nothing says "easy sophistication" like using an expensive handbag when you're ordering a two-piece spicy fried chicken dinner with a side of red beans and rice and a Dr Pepper.

Well, in the winter of my junior year, all my Dooney dreams came true when I finally received "my Dooney" as a Christmas gift. And after that purse and I drove back to Starkville, it made everything better for approximately four seconds when a friend of mine said, "Ooooh, great purse!" But then, in the strangest way, the thrill was gone. It was just the same ole me—only with slightly fancier baggage.

Ultimately that's what materialism does to us. It's a placebo. We think that it's going to make us all better—and maybe for a period of time we tell ourselves it does—but in the end it doesn't improve anything at all.

Because here's the deal: shiny things make lots of promises they just can't keep. Money and possessions don't solve our problems as much as they expose them. They can't fix what's actually broken. But our preoccupation with them reveals that we are all looking to be filled up with something, we are all looking to identify with something, and we are all looking for some acceptance that we think the world and its trinkets can offer us.

There's nothing inherently wrong with nice things—oh, heavens no! The problem is that we turn those nice things into idols (*heyyyy*, "my Dooney"). We elevate them to places of importance they were never meant to hold. So today, ask the Lord to open your eyes to the idols that block Him from your view. Ask Him to help you identify if and how materialism is holding you back from walking with Him. And then thank Him for the grace of a new perspective and a fresh start.

God loves you so much. He gives you everything you really need.

READ MATTHEW 6:19–21.

1. Can you think of a time when something shiny (so to speak) has captured your attention? What was it? Explain.

_____

_____

_____

_____

2. Now that you have the gift of hindsight, do you think you were looking to that thing to fix or change your life in some way? Did you have any acceptance or approval tied up in it?

_____

_____

_____

3. What are some specific ways we can fight the good fight against materialism? How can we stand firm against the idol of stuff?

_____

_____

_____

_____

4. Read 1 Timothy 6:6–7. Write out the verses here.

_____

_____

_____

_____

_____

Today's Prayer

_____

_____

_____

_____

_____

_____

_____

_____

_____

_____

_____

_____

Day 19

$\mathcal{A}$ couple of days ago I saw a Facebook post written by a friend of mine. She volunteers with an inner-city ministry in the city where she lives, and two of the girls she serves had become Christians the night before. The Facebook post celebrated God's faithfulness in the lives of those two new believers, and my friend wrote about what an honor it was to cheer on her new sisters in Christ.

Obviously the post made me smile—and even more so when I thought about my friend's high school years.

My friend's graduating class had a reputation for wanting to do things their own way. They weren't always big fans of authority, and although the class was full of delightful people—some of the most engaging, endearing folks you'd ever meet—their group dynamic could get pretty twisted sometimes. They didn't trust each other very much, and you might even say they battled cynicism.

I know all of these things because I was one of their teachers.

And if you had asked me back then, I would have told you that, based on everything I saw and heard and experienced, I definitely had concerns that some of those kids would self-destruct, that they'd go to college and disconnect from the church, that they'd have little interest in faith or Christian community.

Well, here we are, several years later—and I am happy to tell you that I was oh-so-wrong.

Yes, of course, some remain uninterested in faith. But here's what has happened with many of those former students: they've grown up. In some cases they've crashed, burned, and let the Lord put them back together again. In some cases they've come to know the joys of genuine fellowship and community with other Christians. In some cases they've simply had the courage to live lives committed to doing God's will.

And I tell you all of that to say this: I don't know what hard stuff is going on in your life right now, but *the way it is now isn't the way it'll always be.*

Jesus is always in the business of working out a new and different and redemptive thing.

Maybe you're dealing with a group of friends who can be frustratingly dramatic. Maybe you're passionate about spreading the gospel on your campus, and you feel alone or even mocked. Maybe you feel called to be a light in a dark place, but you're discouraged by the complacency and apathy you see all around.

Hang in there. Seriously. Don't give up. Know that the Lord is working, even if you can't see it.

The way it is now isn't the way it'll always be.

That class that struggled from time to time in high school? Many of them are now world-changers for Jesus. They are loving people, they are serving the lost, and they are making His name known.

So if you or your friends are having a hard time right now—maybe wondering if a surrendered life is worth the sacrifice—let me address those doubts super-quickly: YES. JESUS IS WORTH IT! Trust His leading and His timing.

He's making a way. He really is. Follow Him.

READ ISAIAH 43:16-21.

1. Has there ever been a time when you've been frustrated by stubbornness or immaturity, either in your own life or in the life of someone you cared about? Explain how you felt and how you handled it.

_____

_____

_____

_____

2. When you look back over your life, do you think the Lord has refined you more during difficult times or easy times? When have you grown the most in your relationship with Him? Explain.

_____

_____

3. If you could tell someone only three things about Jesus, what would you say?

_____

_____

4. Is there a hymn or worship song that's a comfort to you when you're discouraged? Write a stanza or two below.

_____

_____

Today's Prayer

_____

_____

_____

_____

_____

_____

_____

_____

_____

_____

_____

Day 20

The most critical unit of time in the life of a young woman is the split-second.

Seriously. It's huge.

Because it's almost exactly how long it takes to make an impulsive decision.

I'm going to explain. But first, a hypothetical anecdote.

When I was growing up, if one of my friends or I had wanted to send an inappropriate picture, we'd have to buy a roll of film first. Then, once we took the pictures, we'd have to finish using the whole roll (if you didn't advance through all the exposures, the pictures were ruined). Afterward we'd have to take the film to a drug store to get it developed, and it would take at least a week for the prints to come back from the lab. At that point getting the pictures *still* wouldn't be guaranteed, because the photo clerks would have called our mamas in a heartbeat if they saw pictures where we, for whatever reason, had neglected to wear our clothes.

For sure the pictures would have been a bad idea to begin with. But ultimately we would have had a week of buffer between the idea and the execution of it, with all manner of speed bumps and guardrails along the way.

These days, though, it's different. And here's where the split-second comes in. We live in an insta-society where we can impulsively snap a picture and send it to hundreds of people in a matter of seconds. That's all fine and good and convenient when you're on vacation and want to send a quick update to the grandparents. It's not so good, though, when you're fifteen years old, holding your phone in front of the bathroom mirror and contemplating taking off your top for the guy in geometry who asked you to send him some nudes.

There's a split-second between taking a picture and sending it. Another split-second between sending a picture and regretting it for the rest of your life.

So if you ever feel tempted to snap or send something you shouldn't, I pray that you'll remember these three things:

1. **Someone who truly cares about you wouldn't want you to compromise your heart, your reputation, or your testimony.** The person on the other side of your text or DM or Snapchat is not respecting you or honoring you. You were made for more.
2. **Don't devalue or dehumanize yourself by becoming someone's pornography.** No one gets to objectify you. No one gets to take what isn't his to begin with. You are a deeply loved and highly favored daughter of the Most High King.
3. **Set up practical boundaries to create margin and protect yourself against the split-second.** Set up photo sharing with your grandmother so that every picture you take shows up on her phone. (I'M SO SERIOUS.) Talk openly with your parents. Enlist a couple of loving friends as accountability partners. Help each other.

Finally, if you've made a split-second decision you regret, don't give it a split-second's more power over you. Don't live in fear or condemnation or shame. Talk to someone. Haul that decision into the light. Soak up God's grace and forgiveness.

You are a treasure, you know.

READ EPHESIANS 2:1-10.

1. Have you made any impulsive decisions that you regret? You certainly don't have to make an exhaustive list, but what did the aftermath of those decisions look like for you? Did you second-guess yourself? How do you wish you'd handled things differently?

2. When you're making a tough decision, whose opinion do you value most? Why is that?

_____

_____

3. Hypothetically, let's say that you're tempted to make a really poor split-second decision. Write out the steps you're going to take to create "guardrails" and healthy boundaries in that situation.

_____

_____

4. Proverbs 11:14 offers sound decision-making guidance. Read it, and then write it down here.

_____

_____

Today's Prayer

_____

_____

_____

_____

_____

_____

_____

_____

_____

Day 21

I am always astounded by the intricate, unexpected ways the Lord connects us to other people and weaves our stories together. Over and over in Scripture we see reminders that we are not meant or made to walk through life alone; the Lord has such a knack for bringing along the right person at the right time.

Early in Luke 1, for example, an angel named Gabriel visited a priest name Zechariah. Zechariah and his wife, Elizabeth, had wanted to have children for a long time, and although they were "well along in years" (v. 7), Gabriel announced that Elizabeth was going to give birth to a son named John who would be special "while still in his mother's womb" (v. 15). Sure enough, Elizabeth got pregnant and Scripture tells us that "for five months kept herself hidden" (v. 24 ESV).

The shock factor of being in her sixties and expecting a baby must have been something else, you know?

Meanwhile, while Elizabeth was "hidden," Gabriel visited her much younger cousin—a teenager named Mary—in Nazareth. He told Mary that she was also going to have a baby named Jesus, and her child would inherit the throne of David (v. 32) and His kingdom would have no end (v. 33).

Mary's reaction is maybe my favorite question in all of Scripture: "How will this be, since I am a virgin?" (v. 34 ESV).

SUCH a fair question, you know?

And right after Gabriel told her precisely how it would be, he shared some game-changing news: "your relative Elizabeth—even she has conceived a son in her old age, and this is the sixth month for her who was called childless" (v. 36).

It was a few years ago when, for whatever reason, that passage seemed to leap off the page when I read it. So I grabbed my pen, and at the top of the page I wrote, "God gave Mary someone who would understand."

Think about it. Finding out that you're going to give birth to, you know, THE SAVIOR OF THE WORLD would be a bit of a shock, but in the middle of that, God didn't ask Mary to walk through it alone.

Suddenly two cousins with a fifty-ish year age difference had way more in common than they could have ever imagined.

- An angel visited Elizabeth's husband. An angel also visited Mary.
- Elizabeth was facing an unexpected pregnancy. Mary was facing an unexpected pregnancy.
- Elizabeth's baby was going to be special. Mary's baby was going to be, like, the special-est. *Ever.*

As C. S. Lewis once wrote, "Friendship is born at that moment when one person says to another 'What? You too? I thought I was the only one.'"

Elizabeth was Mary's "Me too."

After Mary heard Gabriel's news, she "hurried" (v. 39) to Elizabeth's house. The two of them were years apart, but the Lord intricately connected their hearts, their purposes, and their lives.

God is so kind to give us people who can be a safe place. Keep your spiritual eyes wide open as you look for your "Me too." She may not look anything like you expect.

But you wouldn't want to miss her for anything in the world.

READ LUKE 1:5–38.

1. Who would you say is your most unlikely or unexpected friend? Why is that?

_____

_____

2. Do you have a desire to have an Elizabeth in your life? What specific qualities do you pray she has?

_____

_____

3. Do you find comfort in the fact that Mary had Elizabeth—a friend who would understand—in the middle of such unexpected, life-changing circumstances? Why or why not?

_____

_____

_____

4. Why is it good for younger women to have older women in their lives? Are there specific benefits to friendships across generations?

_____

_____

Today's Prayer

_____

_____

_____

_____

_____

_____

_____

_____

_____

_____

_____

_____

Day 22

I adore *To Kill a Mockingbird*. Consider yourselves super fortunate that this is a devotional book, because if it had actual chapters, this is probably when I'd launch into several thousand words about all the things we can learn from Harper Lee's first novel. It is chock-full-o'-truth.

There are lots of *Mockingbird* lines I've committed to memory, but one of my favorites is when Miss Maudie makes an observation about Atticus Finch, a lawyer and father who lives across the street. Miss Maudie is talking with Atticus's daughter, Scout, and she says, "Atticus Finch is the same in his house as he is in the public streets."[1] Miss Maudie's point is that Atticus has integrity. His private self and his public self aren't divided. He's the same person no matter where he is.

Let's talk about that. Because here's what the kids tell me. (And please know when I say "the kids," I'm talking about my high-school girls, but sometimes I like to say "the kids" as if I am 114 years old.)

They tell me that when it comes to social media, sometimes people set up primary, very public, yes-my-parents-know-about-this accounts, and then they also set up a second username that only their friends know about. The second username gets called all sorts of things—a spam account, a Finsta (Fake Instagram)—and it's the unfiltered profile. It's the account someone might use for borderline (or over the line) inappropriate comments and maybe even a little online harassing of a real-life acquaintance or a public figure. In some cases, people use the second account to flirt and share pictures. In some ways, it's a place for social media secrets.

Obviously having a fake Insta, fake Snapchat, or fake whatever brings up some basic questions about who we want to be online and why we think it's okay to be sneaky. There's also something that goes deeper, whether we're talking about social media or behavior on the weekends or adopting a different personality with a certain group of friends:

Why would someone want to divide herself like that?

---

1. Harper Lee, *To Kill a Mockingbird* (New York, NY: HarperCollinsPublishers, 1999).

Seriously. In Christ we have wholeness of mind, body, and spirit. So what's going on if someone feels the need to separate and essentially be two different people? It's the exact opposite of what Miss Maudie said about Atticus, and it reveals a lack of integrity.

So if you sneak around to be a different—maybe more realistic—version of yourself, then it might be good to consider some questions:

1. How would I describe my personality in its most unfiltered form?
2. Is the unfiltered me—the second-profile me—closer to who I really am than I'd like to admit?
3. Does unfiltered me honor God with my words and my actions? Do I love people well as I use that second profile (or as I navigate that different friend group)?
4. Am I ignoring conviction from the Holy Spirit in any way?
5. What are some practical ways to practice wholeness and integrity on and offline?

We're all going to mess up as we work out healthy social media (and real life) boundaries. But when we know we're being double-minded and compromising our integrity, that's a sure sign we need to seek some wise counsel and examine the places where our hearts are divided.

Pray to live and love with your whole heart today.

READ PSALM 86:11–13.

1. Whether you have a Finsta or not, do you have sort of a "second personality" you reserve for certain people or certain situations? Describe what that looks like in your life.

_____

_____

_____

2. Do you find that, given a certain set of circumstances, your personality becomes more cynical? More gossip-y? Maybe even more hateful?

_____

_____

3. Do you ever feel convicted about question 1 or question 2?

_____

_____

4. When are you your best, most whole, most fully integrated self? When do you feel like you are living and loving like the young woman God has called you to be?

_____

_____

Today's Prayer

_____

_____

_____

_____

_____

_____

_____

_____

_____

_____

Day 23

The book of Ruth is the story of a widowed woman named Ruth who pledges her devotion and care to her also-widowed mother-in-law, Naomi. Together they travel from Moab to Israel, and after Ruth starts working in the fields of her husband's distant relative named Boaz, Naomi suggests that Ruth approach Boaz about being her kinsman redeemer (a relative who could step in and rescue a family member who was going through a difficult time). If Boaz agreed, he would marry Ruth and remove the shame of her poverty under Israelite law.

Naomi wanted the very best for Ruth—according to Ruth 3:1, she wanted to "seek rest for [her], that it may be well with [her]" (ESV)—so pointing Ruth in Boaz's direction meant that Naomi was pointing her daughter-in-law toward a better future. She was pointing her toward redemption so that what had been wrong would be made right.

Since Ruth was from Moab, she wasn't necessarily familiar with Israel's redemption process; that's why Naomi gave her step-by-step instructions. And because lists make me happy, I will now share said instructions in a convenient numbered format. Please note that biblical content is in bold, lest you confuse my stream-of-consciousness rambling with the Word of God.

AS IF.

Here's Naomi's to-do list for Ruth's visit to Boaz.

1. **Wash up.** Such an important tip. Wise counsel from Naomi.
2. **Anoint yourself.** I think the gist of this one was "Put on some oil and get that skin looking right, Ruth."
3. **Put on your cloak.** Makes sense. My mama always said that if you look your best, you feel your best.
4. **Go down to the threshing floor where Boaz is.** 10-4. Sort of like meeting him at work.
5. **Don't interrupt his mealtime.** #wisdom
6. **Stay hidden until he goes to sleep and make note of where he lies down.** A little strange, but, um, fair enough.

7. **After he lies down, uncover his feet and lie down too.** Not gonna lie, Naomi. This is straight-up weird to me.
8. **Wait for him to tell you what to do next.** Sounds good. Maybe that will alleviate some of the inevitable awkwardness.

So yes, Israelite customs seem strange when there are a few thousand years between then and now. But we have to remember that Naomi knew the redemptive drill.

And here's something else to consider. Naomi had a voice in Ruth's life, which meant she had the freedom to counsel her and guide her. Naomi knew Ruth better than anyone else; at the point when Naomi told Ruth to visit Boaz, the two women had lived side-by-side for years. Naomi knew Ruth's history, she knew who she was behind closed doors, and she knew, based on the way her daughter-in-law had cared for her, that Ruth was worthy of a man as fine and respected as Boaz.

The takeaway? Even though we're never going to be in the exact same circumstances as Ruth, we all need someone who knows us that well. That level of familiarity breeds trust. And in Ruth 3:5, we see Ruth's reaction to Naomi's instructions: "All that you say I will do" (ESV).

When we trust the older people the Lord puts in our lives, there's little time for second-guessing, arguing, and defiance. Our response tends to be, "Yes, ma'am. You got it." Their wisdom frequently trumps any potential weirdness.

So listen up.

READ TITUS 2.

1. In Ruth 1:16–18, Ruth commits to stay with Naomi during the arduous journey back to Israel (and for the rest of her life as well). What does this level of commitment tell us about Ruth's character?

2. Is there an older believer who has a voice in your life? Who is it?

_____

_____

3. Do the older people in your life sometimes talk about the way they used to do things? What are some older customs that seem strange to you? (And if you don't have older people in your life, you can still answer this question based on what you've seen on TV and in movies.)

_____

_____

4. Read Hebrews 13:17, and then write it out below.

_____

_____

Today's Prayer

_____

_____

_____

_____

_____

_____

_____

_____

_____

_____

Day 24

It's not uncommon to experience what I like to refer to as a spiritual funk. We might feel distant from God, we might be tired of wrestling with a certain struggle, or we might even feel frustrated with the Lord's timing. There are hundreds of different reasons why we might be battling a case of the spiritual "blahs," so to speak, and sometimes trying to work your way out of that place feels like you're walking through quicksand.

One night about three years ago, when I was feeling almost numb about (and stuck in) a situation that was just wearing me ALL THE WAY OUT, I went to my principal's house for a faculty dinner. I would love to tell you that I was super excited about an evening with my friends and coworkers, but honestly, I wasn't. I wanted to stay home and keep to myself and continue to feel numb and maybe even just a little bit bitter. Because you know that old saying that misery loves company? Well, as it turns out, misery also loves pajamas and Netflix and alone time.

When I was in a similar quicksand-y season about eight years ago, my friend Angela spoke some serious wisdom into my life. She told me that when we feel like we can't move forward, we'll do well to *remember*. The Bible consistently tells us to remember what the Lord has done in our lives. "Thank Him for what He has done," she said. "Speak it out loud. *Remember*."

I wasn't thinking about Angela's words before I went to my principal's house for dinner, but after we finished our meal, the Lord provided the most unexpected reminder about the necessity and the importance of remembering.

My coworkers and I were sitting in a circle that meandered around our principal's living room area, and after he encouraged us with a few words, he asked each of us to share something special about the school where we work. I smiled when he made his request, but to be super candid, my heart WAS NOT HAVING IT. I was content to keep sitting in my numb little bubble where feelings were not welcome. Apathy was working fine for me, thank you very much.

But oh, y'all. As people around that circle started speaking, my heart found it increasingly difficult to resist the praise and thanksgiving. Memories ran the gamut from the personal to the professional to the miraculous, and the more I listened, the more awed I was by our loving, faithful God. And when it was finally my turn to share, there was so much emotion churning inside me that I halfway doubted I'd be able to get the words out.

"We don't have any relatives in Birmingham," I said. "So for me, our school has always been family."

That memory was just the spark my heart needed. And as I drove home that night, I made a point to remember. I thought about the joy of serving the kids at our school. I thought about specific relationships that have been so dear and life-giving. I thought about the ways I'd witnessed the Lord at work. And let me tell you: the Lord used those memories to encourage me like crazy. By the time I pulled into my driveway, the quicksand didn't seem quite so deep. The numbness had started to wear off. And before I walked in the house, I found myself praying Psalm 51:10: "Create in me a clean heart, O God, and renew a right spirit within me" (ESV).

So today, whether you're working your way through a spiritual funk or not, *remember*. Think about the Lord's provision in your past. Be assured of His goodness in your present. And anticipate His plans for your future.

He loves you so much. You can trust Him. He is your all in all.

READ PSALM 77:10–20.

1. What are some of your earliest memories of Jesus?

_____

_____

_____

2. Who are some people from your younger years who modeled the love of Jesus and taught you more about Him?

_____

_____

_____

3. When was a time when you were in dire need of the Lord's grace and His comfort? How did He meet that need?

_____

_____

_____

4. You know the old hymn "Amazing Grace"? Write out the stanza that starts with "The Lord has promised . . ." Googling is totally allowed.

_____

_____

_____

Today's Prayer

_____

_____

_____

_____

_____

_____

_____

Day 25

I am convinced—and you'll never, ever change my mind—that music is one of God's very best gifts to us. There's the obvious element of it being fun to listen to—good medicine for our ears, so to speak—but it can also be really good for our hearts and our heads. It can help us clear our minds at the end of a hard day. It can comfort us and make us feel like someone understands when we're walking through difficult circumstances. And it can encourage us and spur us on when we need a little extra motivation.

(It can also, according to some younger friends of mine, help you "get hype," but I don't really know anything about that because hype isn't real high on the priority list for people in their forties. I mean, maybe if Publix has Buy-One-Get-One gallons of skim milk. Because then? WE'LL GET CRAZY.)

About ten years ago I realized that if I made a point to be intentional about what I listened to in the mornings, the Lord used that music to profoundly impact my perspective. If I started my day with music that turned my attention to Him—music that helped my heart and my mind focus on the Lord—it was easier for me to keep my eye on Him and see Him at work during the day's inevitable ups and downs. Giving myself that opportunity for worship was almost like adjusting a camera lens. Making time for praise instead of immediately feeling bogged down by a to-do list had a way of sharpening my focus. It made me more mindful of how I could better love and serve in the different aspects of my life.

So.

It sounds like an exaggeration, but a playlist really can make all the difference in your day. Certainly there's a time and a place for some JT (James Taylor or Justin Timberlake—take your pick), but don't underestimate the power of a morning call to worship—or some reflection on the Lord's goodness late in the afternoon. Because ultimately, making a choice to sing the Lord's praises in the morning—and all throughout the day, for that matter—will remind us over and over again that (1) we have a Savior who loves us and cares for us, (2) our lives are not our own, and (3) He is our biggest priority.

If you have some extra time in the next few days, make a playlist that will inspire you and shift your perspective to your Savior. Those songs won't make your problems disappear, but one thing is certain: music that prompts you to sing praise to the Lord will remind you of what—and Who—matters most.

Listen with your heart. Make a joyful noise.

READ PSALM 100.

1. Is music a big part of your life? Who are some of your favorite artists?

_____

_____

2. What are some of your favorite song lyrics? It doesn't matter what kind of music it is; just jot down some lyrics that you like below.

_____

_____

3. What hymns or worship songs are most meaningful to you at this point in your life? Why are they a comfort or encouragement to you?

_____

_____

_____

4. Write down Psalm 96:1–2. How many times does this verse command us to sing?

Today's Prayer

Day 26

Over the years I've heard of people who celebrate their spiritual birthdays—the day they became a Christian. I've always thought it was the neatest thing, that ability to look back on a specific day and say, "This was it. This was when everything changed for me."

I can't do that though. I mean, I know I was in junior high and at Camp Wesley Pines for a fall youth retreat, but I have no idea what the actual date was. I get that it's not a deal breaker in terms of my salvation, but it would be nice to know. It would even be nice to celebrate every once in a while.

And I wish I'd written it down. I wish I'd documented it in some way.

In the Bible we see that Joshua was a man who understood the importance of marking God's faithfulness. In Joshua 4 he set up twelve stones from the Jordan River at Gilgal. The stones were to remind the people of Israel that God dried up the Jordan so they could cross into the Promised Land. Joshua stacked the stones "so that all the peoples of the earth may know that the Lord's hand is mighty, and so that you may always fear the Lord your God" (v. 24).

And you know what? I don't think we'll ever regret following Joshua's lead.

I'm not saying that we need to all gather a bunch of actual stones and then, you know, actually stack them. But how about making note of significant dates and spiritual milestones in your Bible? Or keeping a journal that chronicles the Lord's faithfulness in your life? Or creating a timeline of pivotal moments in your life and faith? (I actually did the timeline several years ago as part of a Bible study, and it's such a treasure to me.)

Make no mistake: God is good and merciful and just and faithful whether we chronicle our experiences with Him or not. He is no less holy if we don't take time to jot down reminders of His power. But when we document what He has done and what He's currently doing in our lives, we are writing down our story with Him. We are creating a record that will not only encourage us when we re-read it, but it might also encourage a child or grandchild one day. Your handwritten memorial stones might be what the Lord uses to enable a future family member to see that, as Joshua said, "the LORD's hand is mighty" (Joshua 4:24).

Even if your journals stay under lock and key for the rest of time, they'll minister to you when you're going through something difficult or when you just want to sit down and praise the Lord for His kindness in your life. Several years ago, I was waiting on the Lord to answer a specific prayer, and I saw in my Bible where I'd marked a passage that had confirmed a decision and comforted me a few months earlier. In that moment I was reminded that He had answered me before and would answer me again (and sure enough, He did).

We need not ever forget how good God is to us. Write it down so you'll always remember.

READ PSALM 66:1–20.

1. Do you remember when you became a Christian? Write down that story. (And if you aren't a believer, then write down the story of how you decided to explore the possibility of living life with Jesus.)

_____

_____

2. Do you have a favorite Bible verse or verses? Jot down the references here—and then grab a highlighter and mark them in your Bible if you haven't already.

_____

_____

3. Do you ever think about the legacy of faith you hope to leave your children and grandchildren? How could writing down your personal memorial stones contribute to that legacy?

4. If you were to set up memorial stones for the five most significant events in your life so far—times when the Lord has guided you and kept you going—what would those be? (If you can't narrow the list down to five, write as many as you'd like.)

Today's Prayer

Day 21

I am a person who adores a good obsession. I love being sort of endlessly fascinated by something new, whether it's a play or a recipe or a new brand of crackers. And really, I don't fixate on it as much as I just enjoy the fire out of it.

Regardless of what you call it, though, one of my current "obsessions" is a Netflix series called *Chef's Table*. Each episode features a different chef and examines how that chef's background affects his or her philosophy about food and cooking and the whole dining experience. Viewers learn what inspires and drives the creativity behind the cuisine. At the end of each episode, we see a montage of the chef's signature dishes, all stunningly prepared and plated. And because we've been told the stories behind them—not to mention that we've gained some understanding about the chef who created them—those dishes elicit an emotional response.

Whether you're a "foodie" or not, it's downright awe-inspiring to see what people do with the bounty of God's creation. And it's a reminder that when people's God-given talents meet with God's provision, well, the final product is glorious. It is beautiful.

And that's why *Chef's Table* is such a good reminder for all of us.

Here's the thing. You may not feel like it all the time, but God has uniquely wired you to be creative. Sometimes it's in the traditional sense—you paint, draw, dance, sing, build things—but sometimes it's in ways we might not immediately recognize as creative. Maybe you write code or solve equations or create systems in your head. Maybe you make up game plans for soccer or intuitively know how to construct a bridge that won't collapse.

You are creative.

No matter what the specific nature of your creativity may be, you can rest assured that God will provide what you need to exercise those gifts and talents. And because of your background and passions and even your struggles, the product of your creativity will be uniquely you. No one else can make what you make exactly like you make it. It is what it is because it's part of your story.

So when you have the opportunity to be creative today, recognize that using your talent is an offering to your Lord and Savior. Don't let fear hold you back. Don't let insecurities keep you from trying. Thank God for His very good gift, and ask Him to help you use it well. Tell Him that His glory is the desire of your heart. Honor Him with your efforts.

The place where your participation and His provision collide will be something special.

And as you surrender that creativity to the Lord, you'll find that as He is making something beautiful *through* you, He is also making something beautiful *in* you—a humble, willing heart.

That's just something else, isn't it?

READ ISAIAH 45:11-13.

1. What's your favorite creative outlet? How long have you enjoyed it? Can you trace it back to your childhood?

_____

_____

_____

2. What inspires you to be creative? For example, for me it's usually nature or music, but sometimes it can even be something like watching a baseball game.

_____

_____

_____

3. Have you ever recognized that your creativity is a gift from our very creative God? If so, has that realization impacted how you use your creativity to serve others?

4. How can your creativity be an offering to the Lord?

Today's Prayer

Day 28

*H*ave you ever had a friend who almost seems to crave conflict? Someone who is quick to label another person as a bad guy (or girl) or even as her enemy? Someone who casts herself in the role of victim no matter what the circumstances happen to be?

Let's talk about that for a minute. Because the first thing I'd say about that particular behavior pattern is that it's exhausting.

Seriously. It'll wear you out. Because if you're not into keeping score, it's almost impossible to keep up with Conflict Craver's endless list of who's in, who's out, and who's walking a fine line.

It can be super frustrating. Conflict Craver's perception is that there are all these monsters just over the horizon—all these threats just waiting to pounce—but the reality is that there's no one there. The monsters don't exist.

Yet still, Conflict Craver continues to try to hunt them down.

In our flesh, of course, we want to fire back when someone is constantly trying to pick a fight. We want to tell that person all the ways she's wrong, all the ways she's hurting us, all the ways she's damaging relationships. But 1 Peter 3:9 is clear about how we're supposed to respond: "Do not repay evil with evil or insult with insult. On the contrary, repay evil with blessing, because to this you were called so that you may inherit a blessing" (NIV).

(Quick disclaimer: please know that the kind of conflict I'm referring to is someone who frequently *creates* drama and perceives slights where there aren't any. However, if you're dealing with conflict because someone is targeting or bullying you, go immediately to your parents and any other authorities who would have a voice in that situation. That's a whole different deal and in a whole different league.)

Also, pray that C.C.'s heart will soften enough that the two of you can have a conversation about the issue(s) at hand—not an argument, a conversation. And in the meantime, you continue to love (with boundaries!) and show kindness when you can. Remember that we do have a real enemy, but it's not flesh and blood (Ephesians 6:12). So prioritize fighting *that* battle, which can only be fought on your knees, instead of jumping in to one with your conflict-craving friend.

Scripture instructs us "to be submissive to rulers and authorities, to be obedient, to be ready for every good work, to speak evil of no one, to avoid quarreling, to be gentle, and to show perfect courtesy toward all people" (Titus 3:1–2 ESV). We're not going to get that right all the time because, well, *humans* (see also: *broken people*). But the Bible is our standard, right? It's our plumb line; it is steady and true even when we fall short.

So ask the Lord to give you patience with Conflict Craver, especially when you'd rather give her a piece of your mind. Be gentle with her. You probably won't be able to stop her from craving conflict, but, Lord willing, you can remind her that she's loved and bless her with your words.

It's not always easy, but it's the better way.

READ 1 PETER 3:8–12.

1. Do you have any experience with someone who seems to crave conflict? No need to name names, but how did you handle it? Anything you wish you'd done differently?

2. Why is it so hard to respond with kindness when someone (knowingly or unknowingly) frequently stirs up drama or tries to start arguments?

3. How do you maintain healthy boundaries with a friend or family member who tries to pull you into conflict? Explain.

_____

_____

_____

4. Read Proverbs 15:1 and write, doodle, or illustrate it here.

_____

_____

_____

_____

Today's Prayer

_____

_____

_____

_____

_____

_____

_____

_____

_____

_____

_____

_____

_____

Day 29

Remember when you were little and you used to play Follow the Leader on the playground?

You walked wherever they walked. You touched whatever they touched. You jumped when they jumped, yelled when they yelled, stopped when they stopped. And if you didn't do what they did, you were out.

Now that you're older, you probably don't play a lot of playground games anymore. I'm guessing that it would be a rare occurrence for you to get in a line on your way to class and pretend like you're an airplane or maybe even a train conductor. For the most part those days have passed you by.

However, there are most definitely ways that the "follow the leader" premise is still in effect in your life. Think about it, because it can play out in some not-so-great ways:

- Maybe you try something you shouldn't because you think it'll impress a certain social group.
- Maybe you don't stand up for your faith because you're in an environment where you'd be ridiculed.
- Maybe you mock another girl because you're trying to gain the approval of kids you perceive as more popular.

Each one of those instances is a grown-up version of Follow the Leader. Whether it's explicitly stated or not, there's someone in charge of a group, there are unwritten rules, and you have to do what they do or be left out.

And when you play like that, it's not a very fun game.

Fortunately, though, some awesome, now-that-you're-older versions of Follow the Leader can have an amazing impact on your walk with the Lord and your influence on others. Like these:

- Maybe you make a point to listen to some solid, theologically sound teaching every Sunday—and you soak up that pastor's instruction and wisdom.

- Maybe you develop a friendship with someone in your church who's about ten years older and wants to help you navigate this season of your life.
- Maybe you prioritize spending time with Jesus in the mornings so that His voice—through His Word—is the very first one you hear.

Those versions of Follow the Leader? They'll change your life. They'll deepen your relationship with your Savior. They're the kind of following that will teach you what servant leadership really looks like. And eventually—in the Lord's timing and by His grace—you might just develop a desire to lead a group of younger girls in Bible study. Or you might want to organize a local outreach through your church's high school or career ministry. Or you might start to pray that you'll lead within your friend group—to encourage those girls and help create a culture where honor, kindness, and support are the rule and not the exception.

There's a time, 1 Corinthians 13:11 tells us, to "put aside childish things." You've no doubt "put away" the brand of Follow the Leader that reduces you to a mimic. So now that you're older, be sure to follow—and learn from—the ones who follow the only One who really makes a difference.

It's the very best way to learn how to lead.

READ MATTHEW 20:20–28.

1. Who are some leaders you admire? What qualities do they have that you respect?

_____

_____

_____

_____

2. Philippians 2:7 says that Jesus "emptied himself by assuming the form of a servant." What does that tell us about true leadership?

_____

_____

3. Has there ever been a time when you have followed the wrong leader? What did you learn from that experience?

_____

_____

4. Is there a specific area of your life in which you feel a strong desire to serve through leadership? What kind of leader would you like to be?

_____

_____

Today's Prayer

_____

_____

_____

_____

_____

_____

_____

_____

_____

_____

_____

_____

Day 30

*T*here was a time in my life when I was scared of mission trips. For some reason I always imagined that I'd have to stand in the middle of a field and bandage things. And since I am not a person who enjoys medical pursuits, the prospect of traveling to a foreign country and having to serve as some sort of makeshift nurse sounded like the last thing I'd ever want to do.

Sorry, God. I know all about that "go, therefore, and make disciples of all nations" (Matthew 28:19) business, but I don't think I'm cut out for anything involving *sutures*.

My whole way of thinking was crazy, of course. There are hundreds of ways to serve in missions that don't require a person to wear scrubs. But I was afraid, so I looked for a way to disqualify myself.

So here comes the irony. Do you know what I ended up doing when I finally went overseas about ten years ago? *Writing*. I served overseas by *writing*. That trip completely wrecked my perspective and changed my life. However, I would like to point out that one person on our trip fell and had to have stitches, and I did sit with her while she was waiting to go to the hospital—so for the record, I *almost* bandaged something.

In all seriousness, it's high time for all of us—you, me, everybody—to get past this silly mentality that we're not qualified to serve and we can't build houses and everybody knows if you go on a mission trip you have to build a house all alone without any help from anyone and so it's really better if we just stay at home and watch *Gilmore Girls* for the nineteenth time.

You just might need to broaden your idea of how you might be able to serve. And listen, it doesn't have to be on a mission trip, either. You might volunteer long-term with a local organization. You might decide to take a semester off from college and work with a ministry overseas. The point is that *how* you serve more than likely will line up with what you're passionate about.

- If you love kids, serve at an orphanage.
- If you love teaching, help with Vacation Bible School.

- If you love organizing, be in charge of packing supplies.
- If you love sports, organize soccer games for teenagers.
- If you love healthcare, do blood pressure screenings.

Do you see what I mean? You're hardwired the way you are for a reason. And when you surrender your passions to the Lord, you can rest assured that they're going to intersect with someone else's need. Someone will need to be served in a way you're uniquely equipped to provide. I've seen it happen over and over again.

And don't get me wrong. I'm not saying that the Lord won't call you outside your comfort zone. I once found myself playing soccer with a large group of people in Uganda. The Lord is able, y'all.

There's an old saying that the Lord doesn't call the equipped; He equips the called. That is no joke, people. He will equip you for every good work He calls you to do, whether that's here at home or somewhere on the other side of the globe.

Pray for a willingness to go wherever He sends you.

READ 1 PETER 4:7–10.

1. What is your absolute favorite way to serve other people? Do you like working with kids? Cooking for a big group? Praying for individual needs? Whatever it happens to be, write it down.

_____

_____

_____

2. Write down, doodle, or illustrate 1 Peter 4:10.

_____

_____

_____

3. Have you ever thought about how to be a good steward of your gifts? Is that stewardship connected in any way to local or international missions?

_____

_____

4. When you read Jesus' command to "go, therefore, and make disciples," do you think about what that's going to look like in your life? Do you just assume that'll happen on a mission trip, or do you have a different dream?

_____

_____

Today's Prayer

_____
_____
_____
_____
_____
_____
_____
_____
_____
_____
_____
_____
_____

Day 31

So I think we can all agree that we have abundant access to music these days. Like so many of y'all, my iTunes library is chock-full-o'-songs. And although your music provider of choice might be different than mine, I bet we're all pretty grateful for the talented folks who faithfully use their gifts to make our days a little bit brighter. Whether it's a thoughtful lyric, a catchy tune, or an infectious hook that stays in our head long after the song is over, music has a way of helping us express our thoughts and process our feelings.

But as much as I love all kinds of music, I often remind myself how important it is to promote and protect and preserve our connection to one particular genre: older hymns. I know. They're not exactly the Billboard Hot 100. But whether we fully realize it or not, *we need to hear those old hymns. We need to sing them.* They're rich in substance and Truth. And the fact that they've been sung, in some cases, for hundreds of years gives us a point of connection with previous generations of believers, brothers and sisters in Christ, that we'll never know this side of heaven.

This past week at our church we began the service with several newer worship songs that you might recognize, but as we transitioned to the fourth song, I smiled at the sound of familiar chords that I've known since I was a child. As the congregation started to sing, I bowed my head, closed my eyes, and let the words wash over me.

> *Come, Thou Fount of every blessing, tune my heart to sing Thy grace;*
> *streams of mercy, never ceasing, call for songs of loudest praise.*

What an invitation to worship, you know? And thanks to a little post-church investigation (okay, it was really just a Google search, but "investigation" sounds fancier), I can tell you that people have been singing "Come, Thou Fount of Every Blessing" to the Lord since 1758—for more than 250 years.[2] So when we come together in worship and sing hymns,

---

2. "Come, Thou Fount," *Hymnary.org*, accessed March 09, 2017, http://www.hymnary .org/text/come_thou_fount_of_every_blessing.

we're connecting to our Christian heritage. And as we proclaim the Truth in those lyrics, we're also committing the attributes of God's character—qualities that believers were publicly declaring over two centuries ago—to memory.

There's so much we can cherish about all of that.

The last verse of "Come, Thou Fount of Every Blessing" may be my favorite.

> *O to grace how great a debtor daily I'm constrained to be!*
> *Let Thy goodness, like a fetter, bind my wandering heart to Thee:*
> *prone to wander, Lord, I feel it, prone to leave the God I love;*
> *here's my heart, O take and seal it; seal it for Thy courts above.*

There's a profound sense of recognition in those lyrics that we are utterly dependent on God to keep us close to Him and lead us to our eternal home. And in a day when, if we're not careful, we may realize that instead of singing to and about the Lord, we're mostly singing about ourselves, we'll do well to cling to these pieces of our history and incorporate them into our worship.

The only thing good in us is Him. Sing Him hymns of praise.

READ PSALM 95:1–7.

1. What's your favorite modern worship song? What lyrics especially resonate with you?

2. When you think of older hymns, do any particular ones come to mind?

3. Do you have a favorite older hymn? What lyrics especially resonate with you?

_____

_____

4. St. Francis of Assisi wrote "All Creatures of Our God and King" in 1225. We're still singing it almost eight hundred years later. Look it up online and write out a stanza. Think about all the generations that have sung those words over the years. (Isn't that the neatest thing?)

_____

_____

Today's Prayer

_____

_____

_____

_____

_____

_____

_____

_____

_____

_____

_____

_____

_____

_____

Day 32

One day about four years ago, I was in the middle of teaching a riveting lesson about the poetry of World War II when I realized that I didn't feel very well at all. After class I walked down to my friend Anne's office and stretched out on her sofa, and after about five minutes I identified several immediate challenges: (1) convincing my head to stop it with the pounding, (2) managing what had become a raging-hot fever, and (3) conducting the rest of the day's business from Anne's couch—because there was no way I could stand at the front of my classroom and teach.

Somehow, though, I went to my next class, and I tried to teach despite the fact that I felt like hot death. About an hour later I went back to Anne's office, and after she took one look at me, she insisted that I go home. I protested. She insisted again. About twenty minutes later I finally took her advice. After I got home, crawled into bed, and managed to halfway pull up the covers, I fell into a fitful, feverish sleep. When I woke up a couple of hours later, I was so achy that even my fingers hurt. I was so overwhelmed by my discomfort that I actually cried, and I remember being so relieved that I hadn't tried to finish out the school day.

Fortunately, all I was dealing with was a nasty virus that ran its course within about 72 hours. But as I recovered, I kept thinking about my friend Anne and how she could clearly see that something was wrong with me. She wouldn't let me pretend like everything was okay and go about the day's normal business. In the kindest way, she made herself the (very loving) boss of me and sent me home, which was exactly where I needed to be.

And here's my takeaway from that little anecdote: when we're sick or hurting or maybe even so deep in a mess that we can't see our way out, we desperately need trustworthy family members or friends to come alongside us and care for us. Because when we're stubborn about doing things our way, or confused about how to move forward, or maybe even so blind to our current condition that we're not seeing things clearly, we need wise and godly people to lovingly counsel us and point us in the direction of the next right thing to do. As much as we might think that we know what's best, the fact of the matter is that sometimes we don't have the foggiest idea how to handle the issue at hand.

There's no question that it's good to know how to take care of ourselves, to learn to make wise decisions, to be able to confidently handle conflict. Those are great life skills. Even still, there will always be times when, for whatever reason, we just don't make the right choice. We stay with a certain guy even though he leads us away from God. Or we follow a certain friend when she convinces us to go on that make-you-faint diet. We can't discern that something (or someone) has a hold on us, and we can't recognize that we could very well be on the verge of big trouble.

As believers, we're not immune to blind spots.

That's why it's oh-so-important to pay attention to wise people who see what we can't.

READ PROVERBS 15:31–33.

1. When was the last time you let someone step in and help you with a decision?

_____

_____

_____

_____

2. Does it make you feel loved when others try to help you? Or do you tend to resist any sort of assistance?

_____

_____

_____

_____

3. Do you have any blind spots when it comes to taking care of yourself? (For example, I am not the best at making or taking time to really rest.) Who looks out for you when you're battling a blind spot?

4. Write out Proverbs 11:14.

Today's Prayer

Day 33

*W*e Christians love buzzwords. Over the last ten or fifteen years we've heard a whole lot about being *relational, relevant, transparent,* and *authentic.* Those are all good things (even though I would probably be tempted to point out that the gospel is always relational and always relevant—the resurrection of Jesus guarantees that). I one hundred percent understand why people are so drawn to transparency and authenticity. It's fun to meet and get to know people who don't pretend to have it all together, who don't try to convince you that their lives are perfect, and who don't act like everything is wonderful and they don't have any problems and really, they pretty much just walk around under the shelter of a rainbow made out of glitter and awesome. "Real" can be so very refreshing.

However.

A few weeks ago I had a lively post-service conversation with a friend of mine, and she posed some questions that I've been thinking about ever since. "We focus so much on authenticity," she said, "but what about holiness? We're quick to share our struggles and confess our sin, but are we concerned at all with holiness? Or are we just sitting in our sin and then telling people about it and congratulating ourselves with, *Whoa, look how authentic I am?* Are we asking the Lord to enable us to turn away from sin? Are we truly repentant?"

My friend hit the nail on the head, y'all. I can't remember a time in my life when people have been more honest about the particular nature of their struggles, whether the struggle is with food or porn or hook-ups or alcohol or gossip or whatever. That's a good thing since the stuff we leave in the dark will inevitably lead to shame or fear or even greater bondage (keeping sin a secret is never a good idea). We have to be careful, though, that even if we're open about our sin, we don't get complacent in the fight against it.

So if we find ourselves saying things like, *Yeah, I know I shouldn't get wasted, but I just had to blow off some steam,* or *I get that it's wrong to watch porn, but at least I'm not sleeping around,* then we might need to ask ourselves if we truly desire to be conformed into the image of Christ—or if we're just trying to soothe our conscience about a sin that we have no intention of leaving behind.

Please don't misunderstand: I am not saying that we can be perfect. Heavens, no. But James 5:16 tells us to "confess your sins to one another and pray for one another, so that you may be healed. The prayer of a righteous person is very powerful in its effect." Confession is the first step in healing, but *it isn't the healing*. The healing—and the growing in holiness—comes when we're walking in true repentance, when that particular sin has no hold on us and no power over us. That is a work of God's grace and not of our will.

Confession definitely beats secrecy. Authenticity definitely beats pretending. But don't stop there. Move toward repentance, grow in holiness, and walk in freedom.

READ PSALM 32.

1. Is there a certain sin or struggle where you're tempted to rationalize and tell yourself that it's really okay?

_____

_____

2. Have you ever experienced victory over a particular sin? How did that come to pass?

_____

_____

_____

3. Why do you think people are sometimes willing to confess sin but unwilling to turn from it?

4. Read 1 John 1:9 and write it here.

Today's Prayer

Day 34

*I*f there's anything I have learned over the last three years of spending the majority of my workdays in the company of teenage girls, it's that *Gilmore Girls* is the gold standard for television viewing, and no show will ever surpass the wonder of Lorelai, Rory, and Stars Hollow.

Yep. That's the biggest lesson. Top-o'-the-totem-pole, if you will. But if I've learned anything else—especially in terms of things that caught me a little off-guard when I started my job—is that a whole bunch of teenage girls are stressed out. And I'm not talking about occasional bouts of nervousness when there's a particularly challenging test on the calendar. I'm talking about a level of anxiety that is significant and sometimes even debilitating. I'm talking about stress meters that are dialed all the way up to stun.

Sometimes I think about the "why" behind all the stress. It's a little shocking to me, honestly, because I didn't feel anything close to that level of worry and anxiety when I was in high school. And although every person is different, I think several factors contribute to the stress levels I see every day:

1. The year-round parade of extracurricular activities (Nothing lasts for just one season anymore.)
2. The myth of perfectionism (The fact that there's no such thing as human perfection doesn't stop girls from chasing it.)
3. The trap of overachieving (People feel pressure to be a superstar student + superstar athlete + superstar Christian.)
4. The absence of rest (There's little room for sleep when you're pushing to keep up with an unsustainable pace.)
5. The fear of vulnerability (Everybody wants to act like they can manage #1–4 effortlessly, and that of course leads to all sorts of pretending.)

You don't necessarily battle all five of these things at once, mind you, but even one of them can be overwhelming when combined with the steady stream of responsibilities that accompany high school life. Plus, if you're tired and lack a healthy amount of margin in your schedule, it can be emotionally draining to think about how you're going to continue to do everything you feel like you're supposed to do. You're already exhausted from spinning way too many plates, and somehow you have to figure out how to add two or three more.

So here's what I'm going to tell you:

Stop spinning. Set down the plates. If a couple of them break, that's okay. Talk to your parents or a trusted mentor. Tell them what's going on in your head and your heart. Tell the Lord too. Ask Him to give you wisdom and guidance about where to direct your efforts and your energy. Pray. Rest. Listen to music. Watch a silly movie. Hang out with people you love. Take your time.

It's so normal to want to be excellent at what you do. But you can't be excellent at sixteen different things and take care of yourself too. Learn now to prioritize what matters most to you and your family. Learning to set boundaries at this stage of your life will serve you so well in the future.

Anxiety and stress do not get to boss you around, so don't sacrifice your sanity on the altar of achievement. Put first things first and set aside the other stuff. It can wait. It really can.

READ PSALM 61:1-4.

1. Is there an area of your life where you find yourself striving for perfection? Why is that, do you think?

_____

_____

_____

_____

2. Have you ever pushed yourself to the point of exhaustion? If so, what toll did that take on you mentally, physically, spiritually, and emotionally? And if you haven't pushed yourself to that point, then how did you learn to establish healthy boundaries in terms of achievement?

3. If you have a day when you can't do anything other than relax, how would you spend your time? Inside? Outside? Watching TV? At the beach? Explain your dream relaxation scenario.

4. Proverbs 19:21 is a huge encouragement and comfort to me. Write it out here—and then write a little bit about why we can find refuge in those words.

Today's Prayer

Day 35

One of my favorite passages of Scripture is Psalm 77. The psalmist, Asaph, was having a tough time in the first nine verses. He was discouraged, he was weary, he was troubled, and he felt like the Lord had rejected him. He asked some tough questions too:

> Has his faithful love ceased forever?
> Is his promise at an end for all generations?
> Has God forgotten to be gracious?
> Has he in anger withheld his compassion? (v. 8–9)

I mean, I certainly didn't know Asaph personally, but those must have been some dark days, y'all.

However, there's one tiny little word that follows Asaph's questions: *Selah*. It's a word that means "to lift up," and it's also a musical term that means "to accentuate, to pause, to interrupt." It's significant because the psalmist was in a bit of a sadness spiral—he was beside himself in verses 4–9. But then he paused. And after that five-letter word, after *Selah*, we see a whole new perspective in verses 10–13.

> So I say, "I am grieved that the right hand of the Most High has changed. I will remember the LORD's works; yes, I will remember your ancient wonders. I will reflect on all you have done and meditate on your actions. God, your way is holy. What god is great like God?" (vv. 10–13)

That selah—that pause—is almost like an aha moment for Asaph. In fact, Matthew Henry once wrote, "Thus was he going on with his dark and dismal apprehensions when, on a sudden, he first checked himself with that word, Selah."[3] I could even take Henry's commentary one step further: Asaph checked himself before he wrecked himself.

---

3. https://www.biblegateway.com/resources/matthew-henry/Ps.77.1-Ps.77.10

And in all seriousness, there are times when all of us need a little selah. We need a break, a pause, a MOMENT to reflect and remember and recalibrate. Here are three good things to remember when you, like the psalmist, are walking through sadness or difficulty (or maybe when you're just worn slap out):

1. **Remember how the Lord brought you to this place.** His faithfulness and kindness have always been there waiting for you. He has always been training you for the work He is calling you to do. You are where you are for a reason.

2. **Ponder what you've seen Him do.** The Hebrew form of *ponder* is "to have a talk with oneself." Maybe you need to have a talk with yourself about the mighty ways God has worked in your life. Go to Scripture and find verses that remind you of His greatness. Read them out loud.

3. **Follow His way, not yours.** His ways are not our ways, and we should be so grateful for that. Look at verse 13; His ways in your life are holy. He is a great God, and you will never regret following His leading and direction.

One more thing that strikes me about this passage? Asaph said "Selah" after verse 3, but that first pause didn't shift his perspective. He tried again after verse 9. So don't give up. Don't stop pausing. Don't stop "lifting up." You never know when the aha moment will come, but when it does, it's a game-changer.

Selah.

READ PSALM 77.

1. Have you ever been through an emotional or spiritual ordeal that wore you down? Talk about that a little bit.

2. When you deliberately pause in your life—when you *selah*, so to speak—what does that look like for you? Do you like to spend time alone? Go to your room to pray? Go to an especially meaningful place?

3. What's one part of your story that initially seemed random, but now you can see that it was the Lord's holy way in your life?

4. Write out Psalm 46:10–11.

Today's Prayer

Day 36

So I'm sitting here thinking about purity.

Yep. I sure am. Just another wild and crazy night in the suburbs, I reckon.

And the crux, I guess, of all my current purity-related thoughts is that whether it's intentional or not, the call to sexual purity—what you might hear in your small group or Bible study, for instance—sometimes gets communicated with a whole lot of pressure attached. I say that because when I talk to the girls I serve, I have spoken about purity with a whole lot of pressure attached.

Don't burden yourself with unnecessary regrets!
Don't make a bad decision and subject yourself to guilt and shame!
Don't establish unhealthy boundaries and patterns in your relationships!
Don't damage what God has for you and your husband after you're married!
Don't sacrifice long-term peace by giving in to short-term temptation!

Please understand that I'm not being critical of those kinds of statements. There's something to be said for some timely wisdom and even a good, old-fashioned warning. There's truth in each one of the examples I listed; in fact, we could probably sit down together and review each one of those points and nod our heads and look at Scripture and agree that purity is a priority in the life of a believer. No doubt about it.

There's also no doubt that if we think about it long enough, we could come up with hundreds of potential hazards and consequences and worst-case scenarios that result from rebellion in general and sexual rebellion in particular. We could talk until we're blue in the face and maybe even scare each other a little bit.

What I think we sometimes miss, though, in our attempts to encourage one another to "pay careful attention, then, to how [we] live" (Ephesians 5:15), especially when we're talking about a topic that affects teenagers and young adults as much as the pursuit of purity, is this:

God-centered, God-honoring purity brings freedom.

FREEDOM.

THAT IS A BIG DEAL.

However, sometimes (like tonight, when I'm thinking all the thoughts) I wonder if our focus on negative consequences and negative outcomes pushes us in the direction of behavior modification more than it inspires us to be free. Do we try to make ourselves "follow the rules" so that bad stuff won't happen? Or so people won't know that we're struggling? Are we relying more on willpower than the ongoing, transforming work of Jesus in our lives?

Here's the reality: purity most definitely affects the body, but ultimately it is a condition of the heart and mind. Purity is only possible because of Christ's grace in us and our dependence on Him. Purity prioritizes God before self (or another person, for that matter), it prompts us to rejoice instead of regret, and it produces peace not just in the here and now but also five, ten, even thirty years down the road.

Purity won't solve your problems, but oh, have mercy, it sure can prevent a few.

Live and love in the freedom that comes from trusting God and honoring Him with your heart, soul, mind, and body.

Be free!

PSALM 119:41-48.

1. Is purity a topic you think about / pray about / talk about with friends? Are you candid in those discussions?

2. Do you have any personal convictions about what God-honoring purity should look like in your life? What are they?

_____

_____

_____

3. Why do you think young women often battle the temptation to hide their struggles when it comes to this particular topic?

_____

_____

_____

4. Read 2 Timothy 2:22. Write it down here.

_____

_____

_____

_____

Today's Prayer

_____

_____

_____

_____

_____

_____

_____

_____

Day 37

This morning I had a meeting at 7:15, which means that it was about dark o'thirty when I dragged myself out of bed and hopped into the shower. By the time I made my way through my morning routine, added a few items to my bag, loaded the car, and ran our son through a checklist of what he needed for the day, I was a solid 7 out of 10 on the frazzled scale.

Then I realized I hadn't put on my make-up. 8 out of 10.

And then I realized we hadn't eaten breakfast. 9 out of 10.

It was not really the morning of my dreams.

It was around 6:50 when my son, Alex, and I practically slid into the drive-thru at our neighborhood coffee place. After I frantically placed my order, we drove up to the window for what would hopefully be a mercifully fast payment process.

Unfortunately, it was neither merciful nor fast. Plus, I was trying to put on my make-up as we waited for our breakfast, which means my hands were full every time the very kind barista would open the window to hand me something, whether it was a drink or a breakfast sandwich or my debit card. Every thirty seconds or so she'd have something new to pass through the window. After the fourth time I set down my eyelash curler and mascara so that I could grab yet another coffee-related object, I hit 10 out of 10. I was full-blown frazzled. I wanted to mash my accelerator to the floor and spin out of the parking lot and set all my make-up on fire.

But somehow, in the middle of that less-than-stellar moment, a thought popped into my head and worked its way down to my heart:

You're trying to hold too many things.

Considering that I was holding a mascara tube, an eyelash curler, a coffee stirrer, and a debit card, all while attempting to move my car into "drive," that was certainly true on a literal level. And it was equally true on a figurative level. I was trying to get to a meeting *and* get Alex to school *and* run through my to-do list *and* answer a couple of texts—and as a result I felt like I couldn't control my morning. I felt like I was running behind, and instead of taking one thing at a time—moving thoughtfully, deliberately, patiently—I made myself conductor of the crazy train and steered that sucker right off the tracks.

When we're so busy trying to hold all sorts of things—whether that's the result of a hurried morning or a family conflict or a falling out with a friend—we can very easily miss the blessing of the here and now. We can get so blinded by circumstances (or unforgiveness, or bitterness, or a hundred other things) that we miss the blessings that are right in front of us: a few extra minutes with someone you love, the gift of a stranger's friendliness, an opportunity to spread a little joy.

So if you're holding too much today? Lay something down. Put something aside. Let something go. Focus on the here and now, wherever you are. The Lord will meet you there.

READ PHILIPPIANS 4:4-9

1. For whatever reason, running late makes me feel totally frazzled. What does it for you? Being unprepared? Working against a deadline? Standing in line? Something else?

_____

_____

_____

2. In those instances where you do feel overwhelmed by your circumstances, what could you focus on instead? What might help you overcome your frustration?

_____

_____

_____

_____

3. Think about the last time you were super stressed. If you could redo that situation, how would you react / respond differently?

_____

_____

4. Reread Philippians 4:8. What are four or five things from the last week that fall into those categories? Write them down, and then make a point to read them again if you have a moment during the day when stress threatens to steal your joy.

_____

_____

Today's Prayer

_____

_____

_____

_____

_____

_____

_____

_____

_____

_____

_____

_____

Day 38

*I*f there's anything the girls at my school dread hearing from me, it's a good, old-fashioned modesty talk. Because as much as I try to frame any conversation about modesty in a positive way (and keep it light!) (and upbeat!), I would say that more often than not, talking about what constitutes "appropriate dress" makes girls defensive. And I get it. You've heard about the topic so often that it's easy to want to fold your arms and roll your eyes and check out of the discussion altogether.

So I want to challenge you with something today: maybe, instead of making modesty the be-all and end-all, a better focus—a better aim—would be *honor*.

Because let's get this out of the way from the get-go: *there is nothing wrong with your body*. There's nothing inherently sinful about your body. There's nothing indecent or inappropriate about your body. You are fearfully and wonderfully made, and there is no reason for you to carry any shame whatsoever in relation to your body.

Where things can go sideways is when we lose sight of honor in connection to our bodies. For example, for the last few months I've been under strong conviction that how I'm treating my body isn't honoring to the Lord, so I'm making a concerted effort to eat healthier and move more. Scripture says that our bodies are temples of the Holy Spirit (1 Corinthians 6:19), and for the last couple of years you could make a pretty good argument that I've been taking way too much fried chicken to the temple. However, since I very much want to honor what the Lord has entrusted to me in this physical body, I need to step up my game in terms of taking care of myself. I don't have to be perfect, but I do want to be faithful.

The same goes for how we dress—how we adorn the temple, so to speak. When it comes to choosing clothes, do you honor the Lord? Do you honor other people? Do you honor yourself? I'm assuming that you've all heard the "don't cause a brother to stumble" admonition more times than you can count, so I'd remind you that guys are just as responsible for honoring *you* as you are for honoring them. But in addition to that, there are some good questions you can ask yourself when you're getting ready to hit the town, the school function, church, or whatever—especially if you're keeping the idea of honor in mind.

1. Who am I trying to glorify? God or me?
2. If someone needed me to help or serve—with little kids, with elderly people, or with classmates—would I feel comfortable serving in what I'm wearing?
3. If my grandmother saw a picture of me on social media in this particular outfit, what would her reaction be?

And let me be clear: I know that you have plenty of pressures, plenty of decisions, plenty of relational struggles. I don't want to make more of the modesty issue than we should. However, as believers, the issue of honor should always be before us, and we'd be wise to make *that* our priority—in every single area of our lives.

READ COLOSSIANS 3:12-17.

1. Do you put a lot of thought into the clothes you wear? Explain.

_____

_____

_____

_____

2. Do you like for people to notice what you're wearing? Do you like for them to notice you? Or do you even think about it?

_____

_____

_____

3. Is what you wear ever a source of conflict between you and a parent? Why is that?

_____

_____

_____

4. What do you think it means to honor other people with how you dress? Practically how would that play out?

_____

_____

_____

Today's Prayer

_____

_____

_____

_____

_____

_____

_____

_____

_____

_____

_____

_____

_____

Day 39

*I*f you and I were talking over a cup of coffee right now, we could probably name all sorts of pop culture obsessions that have captured our attention over the last few years. Dabbing. The ice-bucket challenge. Memes. There's no way to make an exhaustive list, of course, but if you've ever noticed how something like a dance craze can result in hundreds of thousands of YouTube videos, then you know exactly what I'm talking about.

America, you are something else.

And listen. I have not been immune to pop culture's influence. A year or so ago our family was hanging out with friends before a high school football game, and after watching everybody's kids try to flip water bottles—a big trend at the time—for the better part of a half hour, I decided I wanted in on the fun. It took approximately four seconds for me to realize that I don't have the necessary skills for water bottle flipping, but even still, I was determined. So I flipped and flipped and flipped—unsuccessful each time—until finally, I experienced some clarity: *I am a woman in my forties. I am flipping water bottles at a high school football game. I might want to grab hold of the reins.*

But sometimes that's how we operate, isn't it? No matter how old (or young) we are, we can find ourselves obsessing over something that ultimately matters very little in the grand scheme of things. And while that particular night I happened to be honed in on some 8-inch tall plastic bottles, I've been thinking about other, more serious things that can needlessly preoccupy our thoughts and our time. I mean, sure, there are the standard diversions—TV, social media, celebrity news, the app of the moment—but I think it's good to ask ourselves if we're "obsessing" in ways that take our focus off of what—and Who—really matters. Here are a few:

- the latest gossip
- other people's opinions of you
- money and possessions

- being seen with the "right" people
- being noticed by a certain person

When we find ourselves caught in a cycle of being preoccupied by stuff we know shouldn't matter to us—but for some reason it does—it's always a good idea to place that thing (whatever it might be) under the light of Scripture. What that means is that instead of rehashing gossip, we remind ourselves of the Good News of Jesus Christ. Instead of worrying about what other people think or what they have, we remind ourselves of our identity in Christ—loved, sealed, and secure—and the riches we have as a result of our lives with Him. Instead of strategizing to be seen with or noticed by certain people, we remind ourselves of the joy of being fully known and fully accepted by a loving, holy God.

And listen. Flip water bottles all you want. Embrace the latest viral dance craze. Laugh your head off at the latest meme. There's something to be said for enjoying certain trends that have grabbed hold of the culture. But when you know you're "obsessing" over things that are considerably less carefree—things that come after your joy—talk to someone you trust. Pray for perspective. And let the gospel be your guide.

READ COLOSSIANS 3:1–4.

1. What's your favorite pop culture craze right now? Why do you think you enjoy it?

_____

_____

_____

_____

2. On a more serious note, is there anything that tends to "get a hold of you" in your thought life? Anything that you "obsess" or worry about pretty regularly?

_____

_____

3. If you were to take that thing and place it in the light of Scripture, what would it look like? How would your perspective shift?

_____

_____

4. Look at Colossians 3:2 again. Write it down here.

_____

_____

Today's Prayer

_____

_____

_____

_____

_____

_____

_____

_____

_____

_____

_____

Day 40

There's a passage in Exodus 17 where we learn that the Israelites are going to battle against the Amalekites. Moses told Joshua to round up men to fight, and then Moses said that the next day he was going to climb to the top of the hill and stand with the staff of God in his hand. God had made the staff (picture a big stick) do some wondrous things in the past—pulling water from a rock, for example—so it made sense that Moses wanted his staff at the ready when his people went into battle.

Sure enough, Moses climbed the hill the next day, and Aaron and Hur went with him. When Moses raised his staff, the Israelites did well in the fight against the Amalekites, but when Moses lowered the staff, the enemy began to make progress. Just picture that pattern: staff up = smiling emojis for the Israelites, staff down = frowning emojis for the Israelites.

So it's no wonder that Moses figured out he needed to keep the staff up all the time.

The problem, however, was that Moses was old, and he was weak, and Scripture tells us that his "hands grew heavy" (v. 12). So Aaron and Hur stepped in to help. They found a stone for Moses to sit on, and then they stood on either side of him and lifted his arms. The staff stayed up until sundown, and the Israelites defeated the Amalekites. Even now we can extract some great lessons from the hilltop experience of Moses and company.

Ready?

1. **Remember that you need each other.** Moses could have gone up the hill by himself, but he knew his limitations. You need to know yours as well—and know that it's okay to admit it when you need help and support. Whether you're struggling in school, processing something difficult that's going on in your family, or dealing with heartbreak, you need other people who love you and will help. You don't have to carry burdens alone. Ask the Lord for friends who are strong when you are weak.

2. **Be wise about who walks uphill with you.** You absolutely can be friends with lots of people. But when tough times hit, it's a good idea to keep your circle small. You want friends who are trustworthy, loving, and loyal. That requires discernment and knowing who is best for you in a particular situation. When you're confiding in too many people, you have to rehash what's going on in your life over and over, and that will leave you emotionally exhausted. Be wise.

3. **Remember that your friendships can encourage other people.** If you've ever watched someone love someone else really well— if you've ever seen a family member or a friend meet another person right in the center of his or her need, then you know what an encouragement that can be. When people see you and your friends genuinely supporting one another, it spurs them on like Moses' staff spurred on the Israelites. You'll encourage people you don't even know are watching.

When you're facing difficult times, think long and hard about what friends are going to walk up the hill with you. Then lift that staff. Pray. Accept help from your people.

And trust the Lord for victory.

READ EXODUS 17:8–13.

1. When you're facing a challenging situation, do you immediately run to people? Or do you tend to keep things to yourself?

_____

_____

_____

_____

2. Who are your "uphill" friends? Who are the people you depend on when life gets difficult?

3. You probably haven't had someone help you hold up an actual staff, but when was the last time someone lifted your arms, so to speak? When was the last time someone (or several people) anticipated your need and then met it?

4. Look up Ecclesiastes 4:9–10 and write, doodle, or illustrate it below.

Today's Prayer

Day 41

*L*ast weekend I stayed in a hotel while I was speaking at a conference. And on the day I left the hotel to drive back home, I realized that I hadn't turned on the television one time during my stay. In fact, I think it's safe to say I *relished* the quiet. Because as much as I love it when life is lively, sometimes it all gets to be too much. Between the radio in the car and the ads that blare at me from my computer screen and the auto-play videos on social media—not to mention a job where on most days I talk or listen all day long—the absence of silence is sometimes so noticeable that I feel like it's screaming at me.

Now, I know I can talk with the best of them. I love to have my office, my couch, and my table full of all my happy people sharing their lives with me. But every once in a while, I'm done. I hit my extroverted limit and become the person in a corner who's trying to crawl into the wall so that I can find just a minute to be quiet and think in complete sentences. In fact, there are days when I want to roll down the car window, look around at all the different sources of noise, and greet every single one of them with the loudest *"Shhhhhhhh!"* imaginable.

Or maybe make a suggestion that everyone in my immediate vicinity should play the quiet game.

As much as our culture seems to promote hustle and bustle and noise, however, it's interesting to note that Scripture shows the value of quiet. We see the importance of being quiet and holding our tongue (Proverbs 17:28), the blessing of meditating on the law of God (Psalm 1:2), and the beauty of a quiet spirit (1 Peter 3:4). We know that even Jesus had to be by Himself every once in a while (Matthew 14:23).

So finding time to be quiet, to slow down, to block out the noise—it matters. And for me, setting aside thirty-ish minutes in the morning (after I make coffee, of course) to be still and quiet with God is essential to my sanity (and I'm pretty sure my husband and son would tell you it's a game-changer in terms of my early morning mood). It's a time when I read my devotional book, I read my Bible, I journal, and I pray. I once heard

Beth Moore say that an early morning quiet time settles the authority for the day, and I believe it. For me it's helpful to prioritize that time before distractions and interruptions enter the day.

But just to be clear: quiet times don't have to happen in the mornings. I have several friends who say there's just no way they can concentrate when it's early. My own mama faithfully retired to her room about an hour before bed and had her quiet time then. What's most important is that you're consistently making an effort to spend time with God, and you're putting yourself under the authority of His word *every single day*. You're getting to know Him more *every single day*. You're learning to love Him more *every single day*.

And the fact that your time together with God is quiet? Well, that's just an extra measure of blessing when the world seems so very loud.

Set aside time for Him. Spend time with Him. Be still before Him.

Those quiet moments may very well be the most meaningful part of your day.

READ PSALM 62:5–7.

1. Do you ever feel like you're surrounded by noise? How does it affect you? Does it energize or drain you?

_____

_____

2. If you had to spend an entire day in silence, what would your reaction be? How would you handle it? What would you do with the time?

_____

_____

_____

3. Do you have a regular quiet time with the Lord? How does it impact your relationship with Him? And if you don't have a regular quiet time, would you like to? What gets in your way?

4. Write out Habakkuk 2:20.

Today's Prayer

Day 42

*I*t's just a theory, of course, but I suspect that if I asked you what you want your life to look like ten, fifteen, twenty years down the road, you'd probably list some expectations or goals that are already pretty established. Maybe it's a city where you want to live, or the career you hope to have, or a mental list of your top ten favorite baby names. You might picture yourself living in a modern loft, you might look forward to serving people in developing nations, or you might dream of completing your first marathon by the time you're twenty-five.

The bottom line is that you have some goals, even if you've never spoken them out loud. And more than likely, the to-do list for your future is filled with some good things.

If I may be so bold, though, I'd like to throw out an idea you might not love: *the Lord is not bound by your list.* He's not motivated by it. He's not going to change His plan because of it. He has so much more in store for you than you could ask or imagine (Ephesians 3:20). And sometimes one of the most difficult parts of growing up is surrendering what we think is best for what God knows is best. Sometimes it's hard to let go of what we think our lives are supposed to look like.

I mean, when I was sixteen, if you had asked me what I wanted my future to look like, I would have said that I really wanted to make VHS mixtapes with all my favorite television clips and continue to add to my stirrup-pants collection.

Maybe I should be grateful that His ways are not my ways.

And let me encourage you with this bit-o'-truth: *His ways are so much better.*

A few weeks ago our family was at a high school football game with a couple of other families. As we approached the middle of the third quarter and our team's lead was solidly in hand, some of our friends said they were going to head down the hill to our tailgating tent. My husband and I decided to follow suit about ten minutes later, and by the beginning of the fourth quarter, all of the kids had joined us. We dragged our fold-up chairs into a circle, and as the bands played and the crowd cheered, we must have covered fifteen different conversational topics. The kids wanted to share their opinions about school, the adults wanted to reminisce about their high school days, and we all wanted to chime in about what we like to watch on Netflix.

Can I tell you something?

That night was everything I never knew I wanted.

It was true, genuine community. And the older I get, the more I realize that if we have that—with Jesus at the center of it—then we really do have everything.

So dream big. Absolutely. But hold your dreams in an open hand. Don't get so preoccupied with living an extraordinary life that you miss the blessings the Lord has for you smack-dab in the middle of the ordinary.

It's the very best place to be.

READ PROVERBS 16:1-9.

1. When you were ten or eleven, what did you think your life would be like at the age you are now?

_____

_____

_____

2. Does your life look the way you thought it would?

_____

_____

_____

3. How do you typically react when you don't get what you want? Is it easy for you to have a big-picture perspective (that maybe God's doing something else), or do you get fixated on your circumstances?

_____

_____

4. Has there ever been a time in your life when you can honestly say you're glad—maybe even relieved—you didn't get what you thought you wanted?

_____

_____

Today's Prayer

_____

_____

_____

_____

_____

_____

_____

_____

_____

_____

_____

Day 43

*Y*ou know, when it comes to milestones, the teenage years are chock-full. In addition to the very big deal of a driver's license, at some point there's usually a first date, a first school dance, a first shot at college admissions exams (sorry about that), a first car, and maybe even a first heartbreak. There's high school graduation, freshman year of college, and moving away from home. After you turn eighteen there's the first time you vote, and when you get your first job, there's also a first tax return.

Granted, that last thing probably isn't as much fun as the others, but still: milestone!

Odds are that for the rest of your life you'll look back and recount those big things—those most noticeable rites of passage—but don't miss this: God is intricately at work in the smaller details of your life too. Those moments are also worth documenting, worth celebrating, and worth remembering.

So if you've been praying about something specific, and one morning God clearly answers your prayer through something you read in Scripture? *Write it down.* If you have a friend who unknowingly encourages you in an area where you've been struggling? *Write it down.* If you're watching the sunset with your family and feel overwhelmed by the goodness and grandeur of God? *Write it down.* If you're struck by an epiphany one Saturday morning when you're babysitting someone's kids and suddenly you understand why a certain relationship is difficult for you? *This is a big deal. Write it down.*

When I was fifteen, I went to the drugstore and bought a blue Mead spiral notebook. I didn't really know what I wanted to use it for, but eventually I realized I liked to document my days before I went to sleep every night. I'd write down who I talked to, what I was praying about, what I didn't understand, what I wore that day, what I was excited about, what happened at youth group on Sunday night—pretty much any area of my life was fair game.

It didn't happen overnight, but in time I started to take notice of the Lord's kindnesses in the middle of the mundane. At a point in my life when I probably could have won some prizes for self-absorption, the Lord used that blue notebook to teach me to notice Him. And let me tell you something: when we start seeing the hand of God in the ordinary, everyday stuff, we suddenly find ourselves in possession of the key to genuine gratitude. Because we start to realize that God has ordained every moment of our lives—and in His economy, little is much.

I'm not saying that your Sweet 16 party won't be, like, *the greatest moment of all time.* However, when we make an effort to open our eyes and our hearts, we're sure to discover even more meaningful milestones that just happen to be tucked away in our daily routines.

Write them down. Celebrate. Remember.

READ 1 CHRONICLES 16:8-13.

1. When you think of the big milestones of your teenage years, which one has been your favorite? Or if you haven't experienced many yet, which ones are you most looking forward to?

_____

_____

_____

2. Can you think of something smaller—an unexpected observation or conversation—that unexpectedly encouraged you or taught you something about the Lord?

_____

_____

_____

_____

3. Do you keep a journal? Why or why not?

_____

_____

_____

4. Why do you think it's important for us to celebrate and remember the small things?

_____

_____

_____

_____

Today's Prayer

_____

_____

_____

_____

_____

_____

_____

_____

_____

_____

_____

_____

Day 44

*I*t occurred to me recently that we've probably all had a moment where we've "served" our friends at church as self-appointed Church Critic.

Here's what that can look like:

- "I didn't like the style of music they sang."
- "The pastor was okay, but he didn't really get on my level."
- "Maybe they should talk more about missions."
- "I thought the greeters were a little too friendly."

Most of the time, I really don't think Church Critic has bad intentions. I don't even think Church Critic is trying to be divisive. I do, however, think that Church Critic—whether it's you or me or a friend from school—is actually saying something that goes deeper than a superficial analysis of, say, the worship song line-up. Because when we start to get critical about the way a church service affects us, here's what we're really saying (many times, at least):

"Church didn't make me feel like I wanted to feel."

We go into church and want the service to check off all of our personal preferences. We want to be excited, we want to be moved, and we want to be transported out of our circumstances. But what can happen if we're not careful is that we start to chase an emotion and neglect the part about worshiping our Savior, the one true and living God.

And listen—I'm certainly not saying that emotion in our church services is a bad thing. Oh, have mercy, no. Several weeks ago, in fact, our worship pastor pointed out that it's good and normal to feel affection for God, and because of that, worship *should* be emotional.

What we don't want to do, though, is to manufacture emotion or, heaven forbid, begin to feel frustrated with our pastors if they don't create the kind of environment we think we need in order to experience the feelings we like.

Because at that point, as my mama would say, the cart is driving the horse. We're worshiping our emotional experience more than we're worshiping the God who gave us those emotions—which means that we're teetering into idolatry territory. We're making a little-g god out of how we feel and respond to the service.

And while I can't remember who said it (but it must have been someone really smart), when we're more concerned with how we feel than we are with giving the Lord the honor and glory He's due, then we're not really at church to worship; we're just there to be served.

Let's offer our Savior worship that's honest and real and devoted only to Him. By the power of the Holy Spirit, let's resist the urge to make a church service about our preferences and our opinions and our favorite songs. Let's worship in Spirit and in truth (John 4:24). Let's direct our affections to the Lord as opposed to the fickle persuasions of our hearts. He alone is worthy.

READ PSALM 98:1-7.

1. What are some ways we can respond to church as consumers as opposed to Christians?

_____

_____

_____

2. Why is it important for believers to gather together for worship?

_____

_____

_____

_____

3. Read Psalm 40:3. What does it tell us about corporate worship?

_____

_____

_____

4. Do you worship in song throughout the week or mainly on Sunday? If you worship throughout the week, what does that look like for you? How did you develop that discipline in your life?

_____

_____

_____

Today's Prayer

_____

_____

_____

_____

_____

_____

_____

_____

_____

_____

_____

_____

Day 45

When you're young, it's easy to think that your faith will only impact people who are about your same age. It's easy to assume that you'll probably just share your testimony in youth group or Bible study, and that barring some unusual circumstances, the story of your life (so far) isn't anything that will impact folks who are ten or twenty (or more) years ahead of you.

But not so fast, my friend. I have a (short) story for you.

About twenty years ago I moved to Baton Rouge because, well, I was a newlywed, and that's where my husband lived, and generally it's a solid idea for married people to live in the same place. I didn't know a soul in my new town other than the man I'd just married, and after a lifetime of living in my home state of Mississippi, the adjustment to life in south Louisiana was more difficult than I expected. The culture was livelier, the people seemed more outspoken, and there was a meat combo called turducken that flat-out confused me (Google it). In so many ways, I felt like a fish out of water.

When I started a high school teaching job, I didn't really know what to expect since I'd never taught at a Christian school. I was sick with nerves on the first day. In addition to working in a new place, I also had to master saying all the French-infused last names on my class rosters. The whole experience felt super intimidating, and I wondered if I'd ever feel at home there.

Within a couple of months, though, I experienced two big epiphanies: (1) I'd never been in an environment—as an adult, at least—where Scripture was part of everything we did, and (2) my students made me feel incredibly welcome. It's a strange thing, being an outsider in a school full of people who have known each other for most of their lives, so I was taken aback, really, by how sweetly those kids cared for me. They asked questions about my family, they told me stories about theirs (and not in that way that teenagers sometimes do when they're trying to get a teacher off the subject). They were respectful and hardworking—almost to a fault—and they were disarmingly relational. It wasn't long before I was looking forward to seeing them every day.

And in the most natural, organic way, they started to tell me more about themselves: how they were doing in their relationships with the Lord, what they were learning at church, how they might be struggling, and why they'd learned all the choreography to Britney Spears's latest song. We weren't friends, exactly, because I was their teacher, but we worshiped at chapel services together, we prayed together, and we laughed together.

In a place where I knew next-to-no-one, those kids were like family. Those kids were like home.

They made an enormous difference in my life despite our ten-year age difference. They were willing to be welcoming. They were willing to be open about their faith. And they were even willing to love a new teacher with a super-strong Mississippi accent.

So today, look for the places in your life where the Lord might use you to be a difference maker across generations. He shines in you and through you—no matter how old you are or they are. So reach out to someone who needs some Light.

READ PHILIPPIANS 2:12–18.

1. Have you ever been in a situation where you were "the new person"? How did you handle that? And if not, have you ever thought about what it's like to be a new person in a strange environment?

_____

_____

_____

2. Have you ever thought about ways that your faith could impact someone who's older or younger than you are? List a few specifics.

_____

_____

3. Do you remember a class, a trip, a date, or an event that you expected to be no fun at all, but then somehow it turned out to be a blast? What can we learn from those kinds of surprises?

4. Can you think of some people in your life who might be lonely? List their names here, and pray about how the Lord might have you minister to them.

Today's Prayer

Day 46

We don't get a whole lot of snow here in central Alabama, where I live now. So several years ago, when flurries started to fall one Tuesday morning, schools and businesses quickly dismissed so that people could get home before the worst of the snow started to fall after lunch.

The only problem was those initial flurries froze as soon as they hit the pavement. Nobody realized that, of course, until half of Birmingham was getting on the roads at approximately the same time, and within half an hour drivers were trapped in a massive gridlock. I was on the way to pick up my son at his school when I realized that there was no possible way my car could navigate all the hills along my route, so I turned around about a mile away from my work.

Over an hour later, I finally made it back where I started. And since cell towers and phone lines were completely overloaded, I couldn't get in touch with my husband or our son's school. Email was the only way we could communicate, and after a couple of hours we realized that all three of us were going to be stuck at our respective spots for the night: me in my classroom, my husband at his office, and our son at his school.

Needless to say, it was a surreal day. In fact, just last week our family was talking about it as we drove from church to lunch, and we revisited some of the stranger details: how I mostly drove on the shoulder of the road so my car wouldn't slide so much, how our neighbors rescued us the next day, how people abandoned their cars in the middle of the road so they could walk to safety. Alex mentioned that he remembered every detail of what many of us now refer to as "Snowmageddon."

And after a few seconds of silence, he piped up again from the back seat and said something more profound than he even knew: "It's weird how we remember the bad stuff almost perfectly, you know?"

Yes. Yes, we do. And that is why I want to be sure to say this to you:

I don't know what your "bad stuff" has been. I don't know if it's something you did or something someone did to you or something that no one could have controlled even if they tried. But I know the mental and emotional agony of rehashing a decision or a conflict or a heartache. And I know how we have a tendency to keep some of the worst moments of our lives filed away in the back of our minds, ready to pull them out of the archives at any moment and press "play" so that we can relive the sadness, shame, or sorrow all over again.

But don't you forget that the saving grace of Jesus Christ means that we don't have to live in the wasteland of our "bad stuff." We don't have to live as grief's prisoner. We don't have to live like the person we used to be.

Because of the blood of Jesus, forgiveness, freedom, and healing are available to us. He's not disappointed or angry with you. He will never withhold His love from you. There's no need to relive the past when He is the One who secures your future.

That storm you keep replaying in your head? It's over. Rest in the loving arms of your heavenly Father, where you are forever safe and sound.

READ PSALM 103:6–14.

1. Is there anything from your past that you tend to put on replay (and then rethink and reevaluate and maybe even regret)?

_____

_____

_____

2. Has that event affected the way you see yourself? Or the way you think the Lord sees you? Explain.

_____

_____

_____

_____

3. Look at verse 11 of Psalm 103. What kind of love does the Lord have for those who fear Him?

4. Look up the definition for the answer to question #3. Write it down here.

Today's Prayer

Day 41

A friend of mine owns a beautiful breakfast room table. It's custom-made, large enough for her whole family, and weathered in such a way that it looks loved instead of worn. It's one of those pieces of furniture that people pass down to the next generation, and it will no doubt serve my friend's family members for years to come.

There's only one problem, though.

About six months ago, my friend realized the table was warped.

It *looked* fine—you wouldn't have known anything was wrong with it if you just glanced at it—but if you sat down to eat at that table, it only took a few seconds to realize, *Oh, I do believe that something has gone awry; the center is sinking. This table is starting to resemble a very large bowl.*

What I find so interesting about my friend's table is that such a subtle problem—one you couldn't even see from across the room, one that happened very slowly, over a period of time—well, it completely affected the table's usefulness. Even though it looked fine, it couldn't work like it was supposed to work because anything around the perimeter of the table was likely to slide to the middle.

You can understand why that was a little inconvenient if someone was trying to serve a meal.

You can also understand that you and I have more in common with that table than we might realize. The table's subtle, gradual warping is exactly what sin, left unchecked, will do to our hearts. We may think that we're only moving the tiniest step away from God's best for us—that it's no big deal, really, if we shimmy a little bit away from the invisible line that separates His will from ours. *How* we shimmy and *why* we shimmy will be different for everyone, of course. In some cases it's crossing boundaries with a boyfriend because we're tired of fighting temptation, or it might be going against your parents' wishes because you want to hang out with your friends. Or maybe it's stealing. Maybe it's lying. Maybe it's cheating over and over again in a class that frustrates you to no end.

And here's what's tricky: a series of small compromises won't necessarily make us look any different to the people around us. Over time, though, we'll realize that we can't serve as effectively as we'd like. The enemy will come after us with shame, or our sin will affect our relationship with God, or we'll start to isolate ourselves in the hopes that no one will see what's really going on.

Once my friend realized her table was warped, she immediately contacted the person who made it so that he could identify the problem and make the necessary repairs. The same strategy applies to you and me too. When we realize that something is "off" in our relationship with the Lord, we need to go to the One who made us, admit what's going on, and ask Him to help us. Because He's gracious and loving, He'll convict us through His Word and by the power of the Holy Spirit. He'll forgive us. He'll set us back on the right path.

And we can serve in the ways we're designed to serve.

READ PROVERBS 3:1–12.

1. Can you think of an object that can look totally normal when it's actually in no condition to do the job it was designed to do, like a dull knife or a pen with no ink? What are some that occur to you?

2. When was a time you looked normal to the people around you, but based on what you were dealing with emotionally or spiritually, you knew that their perception and your reality were totally different?

3. If you had to identify the areas where you're most tempted to compromise, what would you list?

_____

_____

_____

_____

4. Read 2 Timothy 1:9. Write it down here.

_____

_____

_____

Today's Prayer

_____

_____

_____

_____

_____

_____

_____

_____

_____

_____

_____

_____

_____

Day 48

*M*y Mama and I talked for the last time a week before she died.

We didn't know it was our final conversation this side of heaven, of course. I'd called to check on her and Daddy, and while she didn't normally like to talk on the phone very much—she'd been diagnosed with dementia, which really affected her speech and processing—she was definitely up for a conversation that Monday night. It took a lot of effort and energy on her part, but for about ten minutes she asked and answered questions, she laughed, and then I could tell she was ready to tell me good-bye.

"All right, Mama," I said. "I'll talk to you later. I love ya."

And although her speech was very slow, her response was loud and clear. "Love you too," she said.

Four days after that phone call Mama woke up Daddy in the middle of the night and told him she was having trouble breathing. By the time an ambulance got her to the hospital, she had stopped breathing. The EMTs eventually revived her, but she never woke up, and three days later she passed away. Our family continues to find great comfort in knowing that she is whole and free, that she has met Jesus face-to-Face.

None of that, however, changes the fact that I miss my mama. I don't think that feeling will ever go away. And I want to be sure to tell you something that has crossed my mind countless times since she died: *Of all the sweet things my mama said to me, that final "Love you too" absolutely means the most.*

Mama and I didn't have a perfect, Lorelai and Rory-ish mother-daughter relationship. We loved one another deeply, but we were different in many ways. Mama was gentle and patient and reserved; she kept many of her thoughts and feelings to herself. I am strong and stubborn and outspoken; I've kept approximately four feelings to myself over the course of my whole life. Mama and I shared great affection for faith, family, and home, but occasionally it was hard for us to understand each other because our personalities were so opposite.

Mama's dementia diagnosis, though, threw everything in perspective. When I was with her, I tried to slow down—whether that was to help her into bed at night, to rub her legs when they ached, or to sit with her at the table as she lingered over her breakfast. The little things that had always mattered so much to Mama suddenly mattered a great deal to me because I knew our time together was precious. I had always adored her, but it became very important to adore her in the ways that spoke to her—not the ways that came most naturally to me.

Bottom line: you may not have as much time with your parents as you think. Scripture tells us to obey our parents and honor them (Ephesians 6:1–2). That doesn't mean we're always going to agree. But when it is possible (and sometimes it's not because of circumstances beyond your control), love them well. It's so easy to take the moments and the days and the months together for granted. Truly, though, you don't know when a conversation might be your last.

So remember: lots of *I love yous*. Lots of compassion. Lots of grace.

It's the very best way—because it's His way.

READ 2 CORINTHIANS 13:11–13.

1. Have you ever experienced the death of a family member or close friend?

_____

_____

_____

2. What did the Lord teach you in or through that relationship?

_____

_____

_____

3. Is it important to you to be at peace with the people you love? To know there's no lingering tension or resentment? Explain.

_____

_____

4. Do you try to have a "no regrets" policy in your relationships with family members and friends? Why or why not?

_____

_____

_____

Today's Prayer

_____

_____

_____

_____

_____

_____

_____

_____

_____

_____

_____

Day 49

We've always been sports fans in our house, but because of our deep and sincere allegiance to college football, we've never paid much attention to the NFL. I've never really been able to keep all the teams and mascots straight. And even though I've been familiar with a few of the higher-profile players, my interest level in all the regular season shenanigans has been somewhere between minimal and ain't-nobody-got-time-for-that.

But last year, well, SOME THINGS CHANGED.

A former, much-beloved Mississippi State player was named the starting quarterback for the Dallas Cowboys (in his rookie season, no less), and that was all it took for my interest in the NFL to ramp up to, *Now where exactly do I purchase my Cowboys T-shirt?* I went from not even knowing the name of the Cowboys' coach to being able to recite who's on the injured reserve list. I won't go so far as to say that the Cowboys have become a consuming passion for me, but I *am* considering painting my kitchen the color of their home game uniform pants.

Make of that what you will.

And now that I'm awash in all my newfound Cowboys knowledge—even going so far as to follow the team on social media—there is something that has really impressed me. Week after week, former players get on social media and encourage the younger players. It might be something as simple as a quick comment after a great play or an affirmation that So-And-So is going to be a legendary cornerback or an assertion that a rookie defensive lineman is the real deal.

By and large the retired players aren't negative, they're not pointing out mistakes, and they're not pounding their chests and listing all the ways their team was better.

They're just watching the younger guys play, and they're cheering them on.

I'll be totally honest with you. It fires me up a little bit. In a good way, I mean. Because there's something about seeing the generation ahead look at the generation behind them and say, in so many words, *You've got this!*

You're awesome! It brings me joy to watch you play! In fact, it sort of makes me want to strap on some shoulder pads, lace up some cleats, and hit the field.

When you get right down to it, *this is what we all should be doing.* We should have an eye on the generation behind us, and we should absolutely be their biggest fans in terms of encouraging them to use the gifts the Lord has entrusted to them. Sure, we could sit around and talk about how if we'd been able to sing like that when we were eleven years old, we'd have for sure been the next Taylor Swift or whatever. We could make all sorts of claims about how our age group did this thing better or worked harder or knew what it meant to have to fight for every single opportunity.

Or we could stop talking about what-ifs and focus on what is.

There's a generation behind you that needs to be encouraged and affirmed for the unique ways they love and serve and play and sing and dance and write and create. Consider how the Lord might want you to cheer them on today.

READ 1 THESSALONIANS 5:12-24.

1. Think about the people who consistently cheer you on. Are they older, younger, your own age? What does that say to you?

2. Think for a minute about some younger people who might just love some encouragement. Write down their names, and then think about how you'd specifically like to encourage them.

3. Have you ever felt threatened by someone who's younger than you are? I'm not talking about physically, of course! I'm talking about being threatened by their abilities, by believing that somehow they're going to overshadow you. What's the danger of this way of thinking?

4. Why does it mean so much more to us when we're affirmed by someone who's older than we are? What makes that so special?

Today's Prayer

Day 50

Whether you've grown up in church or not, you've probably heard the phrase "salt and light" a few times. It comes from a section of Jesus' Sermon on the Mount, and it speaks to the way Christians should live. First, we're supposed to be salt, which means that our words and our actions should preserve the Truth of the gospel in a sinful world. Our saltiness, so to speak, can also enhance how we interact with people on a day-to-day basis, whether that's in our conversations, our reactions to authority, or our care for the lost and the lonely. And then as lights, we should shine in a world of darkness; our lives should be beacons that point others in the direction of our Savior.

From a gospel perspective, that all makes great sense, right?

However, being salt and light can be challenging. For one thing, we live in a world that is increasingly resistant to (1) Christianity, (2) the church, and (3) Christians. And on top of that, we're all dealing with stuff in our own lives that can sometimes make it difficult to walk the salty walk, so to speak.

So, if I may be so bold, I want to point out five things that—if left unchecked—will kill our FLAVA (you're welcome) and dim our lights.

Ready? Here we go.

1. **Unforgiveness and bitterness.** I'm gonna shoot straight here: we can't hold something against another person and then expect our lights to shine as if unforgiveness is no big deal. Like it or not, our unforgiveness makes us cynical and ineffective. It casts a shadow not just over our own hearts and testimonies, but also over the body of Christ.

2. **Self-Righteousness.** We really can't underestimate how acting morally superior spoils the salt and puts out the light. *There is no room for it.* There's a great big hurting world out there, and I can promise that people outside the church don't want to hear about how perfectly holy we're all pretending we are. We need to get real.

3. **Compromise.** We cannot live our lives sitting on the fence and expect to have kingdom impact. And I'll be totally honest: the older I get, the more I think that compromise is cowardly. It's a refusal, ultimately, to take a strong stand on either side. We don't want to be legalistic. But if we claim that our lives are about one thing—Jesus—while openly living in a way that contradicts that, we lose our voice with people.

4. **Shame.** May I just remind you of something? Whatever that thing is that you have a tendency to carry around? That guilt or that insecurity or that lie that just holds you in its grip? Lay it down. Tell somebody. Read Psalm 103:11–13. And take Him at His word.

5. **Apathy.** Be careful when you start to feel like a quiet time doesn't matter. Or that confession and repentance don't matter. Or that prayer and worship don't matter. Because apathy is a Great Big Flava Killer. And as long as we have the gospel, we have Great Big Hope.

You're called to be salt and light in this world for His name's sake. Remember that God made you to season and to shine.

READ MATTHEW 5:13–16.

1. Can you identify any places in your life where you're struggling with unforgiveness? Are you holding any grudges or dealing with any bitterness?

_____

_____

_____

_____

2. What are the areas of your life where you're tempted to compromise? Are there areas or issues or behaviors where you know what the Lord says, but you still want to follow your own way?

_____

_____

3. Are you apathetic about anything? Have you ever found yourself saying something like, *I know I should care, but I just don't?*

_____

_____

4. Read Psalm 51:10. Write, doodle, or illustrate it here.

_____

_____

Today's Prayer

_____

_____

_____

_____

_____

_____

_____

_____

_____

_____

<h1 style="text-align: center;">Day 51</h1>

I can't think of a time in my life when young women have had more activities piled on their proverbial plates. There's school, of course. There are extracurricular activities—drama, band, debate, student government, sorority, you name it. There are sports, and for many folks that means a school team and a league or travel team. There are part-time jobs. There are responsibilities at home. There are regular workouts at the gym. There are dance lessons and voice lessons and college entrance exam classes. There are Bible studies and youth groups and mission trips and church camps. And then there's homework and studying, which, according to most of the girls I talk to, can be an overwhelming task at times.

Plus, somewhere in the middle of all of that, there's supposed to be a social life. Family time. Quality time with friends.

And when you start to consider not just the number of activities that high school and college-aged girls are supposed to cram into a given week, but also the intensity and the demands of those activities, well, you can't help but jump to the conclusion that most girls between ages fifteen and twenty-two can sleep two nights a week for approximately four hours each. But that's it. That's all the sleeping the schedule will allow.

It seems like a crazy amount of responsibility to carry, right? But at the same time, it's the reality for a whole lot of people. And for the most part, lots of people who are maintaining these sorts of schedules are doing everything they can to honor the Lord with their excellence and their efforts. They're conscientious, they're high-achieving, and they're trying to give all of their various interests everything they have.

That's why I almost hate to bring up this tiny dose of reality for fear that it may seem discouraging.

But I'm going to say it anyway.

You really can have it all, motivated people. You really can.

But you absolutely, one hundred percent cannot have it all AT THE SAME TIME.

It's not possible. Nobody is built to run at the kind of pace that so many high school and college girls are running. It's not sustainable. It's not healthy. It's not wise.

And there's a legitimate spiritual danger in the mix, too, because you can do all of these things and try to prioritize all these things and love all of these things and commit all these things to the Lord—and then miss the Lord entirely. Seriously. You can be so busy managing your schedule and trying to achieve your goals and essentially reducing your life to an exhausting list of what you "need" to do that you miss the sacred, every day joys of spending time with Jesus. Of abiding. Of sitting at His feet, so to speak, and talking with Him. Listening to Him. Slowing down long enough to rest in Him.

So as you consider the next stage of your life, as you pray about where to direct your attention and your efforts, ask the Lord to make you aware of your deep need to seek Him above everything else. It won't be anything you list on a résumé, it won't elevate your GPA, and it may mean that a few things you want to do have to take a backseat for a season. But you'll never regret the peace of walking in growing intimacy with your heavenly Father.

Ultimately He is the only "all" you need.

READ LUKE 10:38-42.

1. Do you ever feel over-involved or over-programmed? Explain.

_____

_____

2. Are there certain activities that you think you *need* to do even though you don't *want* to do them?

_____

_____

3. How important is "down time" to you? Do you prioritize it? Or do you feel lazy if your day isn't scheduled to the max?

4. Do you identify more with Mary or with Martha? Explain.

Today's Prayer

Day 52

When I was a freshman in college, I met a group of girls who remain some of my closest friends. Our bond was instant, and it has been lasting. We might not see each other as much as we'd like, but when we do get together, we pick up right where we left off. There's a connection between all of us that defies distance and time.

About ten years ago, one of those friends experienced a terrible loss. It was a tragedy that compelled the rest of us to travel so we could be with her. All of us spent about five days together around the clock. And when it was time for me to go home to Birmingham, I got in my car, drove about ten miles, and began to cry so hard that I wondered if it might be wise to pull over on the side of the road. I knew that I needed to be with my family—ultimately I *wanted* to be with them—but after everything my friends and I had been through together (and as sweet as the Lord had been in our midst), I craved the constant comfort and understanding I'd felt when I was with them.

I don't think it's unusual to experience something deeply emotional and spiritual and then want to stick close to the folks who walked that road with you. It's hard to figure out how to transfer something life-altering from a private group where you feel safe and protected to a more public environment where you might feel raw and vulnerable. Sometimes it's tempting to stay close to the shelter even after the storm has passed.

We see a similar situation in Scripture. In Mark 5, Jesus healed a demon-possessed man. Word spread quickly about what Jesus had done, and when people came to see for themselves, they saw the formerly possessed man "in his right mind" (v. 15). It must have been shocking. When Jesus got ready to leave, the man He had healed begged to go with Him. No doubt he wanted to stay close to his Healer and the safety of that spot.

However, Mark 5:19–20 says that Jesus "did not let him but told him, 'Go home to your own people and report to them how much the Lord has done for you and how he has had mercy on you.' So he went away and began to proclaim in the Decapolis how much Jesus had done for him, and they were all amazed."

What a reminder that is. As miraculous as it can be to see the Lord at work in the middle of difficult circumstances, we can't camp out in that place indefinitely. We're meant to keep moving forward, to keep growing in our faith, and to keep sharing what we've seen Him do.

Yes, there's something sweet about a safe place. Those places serve us well in certain seasons. But eventually we're called back into the real world so we can testify to the Lord's mercy and faithfulness, and so others will be amazed.

If you or your friends are dealing with something difficult, be brave when you're in the middle of it and love each other really well. But also be brave enough to share the story after the storm has passed. The Lord's mercy is enough to carry you through both.

READ MARK 5:1–20.

1. Who are the people who become a safe place for you in the middle of something difficult?

_____

_____

2. Think about the way you bond with people when you go through something tough together. Why is it so hard, do you think, to re-enter real life when you've been cocooned with certain people or in a certain environment?

_____

_____

_____

3. Jesus isn't being rude when He tells the man who's no longer possessed to "go home." What are a few reasons why going home is the wise thing for the man to do?

_____

_____

4. Why do other people need to hear about the times when the Lord has been merciful to us? Write down the first three or four ideas that come to mind.

_____

_____

Today's Prayer

_____

_____

_____

_____

_____

_____

_____

_____

_____

_____

_____

Day 53

*A*t some point most of us have longed for true friendship. Since we are hard-wired for community, we want to be known and understood. These are good, God-given inclinations. We can get in trouble, though, if insecurity and desperation start to enter the picture. Because when we get insecure and desperate, we sometimes allow unhealthy people to have access to our hearts and minds. And I'm not talking about people who are physically unhealthy. I'm talking about people who are emotionally unhealthy: manipulative, controlling, and self-absorbed.

Those people will *wear you out*.

Several years ago I talked with a friend whose daughter was having friend trouble. The daughter felt like the person she'd considered her best friend had changed in recent months. The supposed best friend seemed to specialize in critical comments, whether she was talking about people she didn't know or my friend's daughter's clothes or a classmate's haircut. My friend's greatest concern was that her daughter was trapped in a bad friendship, and after I listened to a few stories about how the supposed best friend had treated my friend's daughter, how she had undermined her with other girls and even gone so far as to start rumors about her, I'd heard enough.

"Hey," I interjected. "Based on what you've said, that girl isn't your daughter's friend. She's more like a mob boss. Their relationship isn't about friendship; it's about control."

And really, it's easy to let the dynamics of a friendship get away from you, particularly if some unhealthy patterns start to take hold. That's why it's good to remember that genuine friendship isn't about control or manipulation, and it certainly isn't rooted in fear. It is a beautiful gift from God, and here are some ways we can know if it's the real deal:

1. **You're loved just as you are.** This doesn't mean you're perfectly awesome and there's absolutely no room for growth in your life. It does mean, however, that who you are at this particular

moment in time is enough. You are *not* someone's project, and you do *not* have to complete anyone's checklist in order to be accepted. Your heart is safe and at home.

2. **You laugh. A lot.** When I meet with girls who are having trouble with friends, one of the first questions I ask is, "Do you laugh together?" If the answer is "no," then the odds are strong that the friendship isn't long for this world. Laughing together creates a bond. It becomes a shared language and marks significant moments on the time line of your history together.

3. **You're encouraged and supported.** A good friend will tell you the truth and cheer you on in the ways that matter most. That friendship won't come between you and your parents, it won't interfere with your faith, and it won't lead you in the direction of regret. Instead, you'll be affirmed in your gifts and appreciated for your uniqueness. The unconditional support of a true friend will boost your confidence and your courage.

True friends are a blessing from God; give thanks for them today!

READ PROVERBS 22:24-25.

1. Do you have a friend who consistently encourages you and spurs you on in your relationship with Jesus?

_____

_____

2. Have you ever been in a friendship that you knew was unhealthy? How did (or does) that relationship affect you?

_____

_____

_____

3. What qualities are most important to you in a friend? Do these qualities line up with Scripture? Look specifically at Galatians 5:22–23.

4. How could you be a better friend? Are you able to identify any ways that you could be more Christlike in your relationships?

Today's Prayer

Day 54

$\int$o here's a cheerful thought for you this morning: *You have an enemy, and he is a liar.*

I know. It's not exactly the most upbeat declaration. But it's the truth. And what we don't always realize is how much the lies of the enemy inform and affect our decisions.

In fact, I'd go so far as to say that every poor choice we make is rooted in one of the enemy's lies. He dangles a counterfeit "truth" in front of us, and we grab for that thing just like it can rescue us.

Here are some examples.

- The enemy tells us that what Christ did for us on the cross isn't enough, so we buy into the lie that we have to be perfect (and create an elaborate façade so it looks like we are).
- The enemy tells us our worth is based on how we look, so we micromanage our eating and exercise to the point of unhealthy obsession.
- The enemy tells us we need the attention of a guy to define us, so we compromise our hearts and our bodies to try to hold on to someone who shows interest.
- The enemy tells us people can't be trusted, so we sabotage relationships before someone has the opportunity to hurt us.

We could go on and on.

The biggest mistakes of my life have been because I not only believed the enemy's lies, but I also acted on them. In situations where I could have run toward the light of Christ and His promises, I chose to operate out of fear. I heeded the enemy's insistence that the Lord would not come through for me, that my circumstances would overwhelm me, and that my disobedience and compromise wouldn't matter as long as other people didn't find out.

Lies, lies, lies.

The harsh reality is that believing the enemy's lies can lead us into all sorts of bondage. And no matter what form that bondage takes—drug addiction or cutting or bulimia or sexual immorality or countless other things—getting free from it can be a long and treacherous process. That's why it's critical for us to remember that our freedom is in the Truth. God's Word will never steer us in the wrong direction, and it will never push us toward regret or humiliation or shame. It is always a sure and steady compass.

And when you are tempted to listen to the subtle, deceptive voice of the enemy, consider Isaiah 54:17: "No weapon that is fashioned against you shall succeed, and you shall refute every tongue that rises against you in judgment. This is the heritage of the servants of the LORD and their vindication from me, declares the LORD" (ESV). If you belong to the Lord, you have authority in the name of Jesus to rebuke and resist the enemy's lies. Tell him to BACK OFF in the strong name of Jesus. Replace his lies with the Truth of Scripture.

Walk in freedom today.

READ EPHESIANS 6:10–20.

1. Is there any particular lie that you find yourself battling over and over again?

2. What have been the consequences of that lie in your life? Has it robbed you of confidence? Influenced some decisions? Resulted in some regret? Explain.

3. Fill in the blanks as they apply to your personal struggle(s):

   The enemy says I am _____.

   The Lord says I am _____.

4. John 10:10 reveals that the enemy has three primary purposes. What are they? How does this verse reinforce the fact that he is not to be trusted?

_____

_____

_____

Today's Prayer

_____

_____

_____

_____

_____

_____

_____

_____

_____

_____

Day 55

*L*ast night a friend and I were talking about how we sometimes get tripped up when we have to adjust our expectations. You can probably relate to how this happens. Maybe what you thought was going to be a quiet weekend at home turns into a situation where you have three tests on Monday, or maybe what you thought was going to be a low-key night with girlfriends becomes a full-fledged counseling session because someone is having a hard time. Maybe it's just that you hoped to have a no-obligation afternoon and then realized you needed to complete approximately 391 scholarship applications. The point is that we have a tendency to get unsettled and maybe even annoyed when things don't go according to our plan.

And here's the kicker: life very rarely goes according to our plans.

This can be disconcerting because, well, we are generally fans of our own plans. We tend to think that our days should play out just as we want, so when inconveniences and interruptions arise, we balk a little bit. We might even whine.

As my friend and I discussed how we struggle with loosening our grips on the reins, so to speak, I realized that one word kept creeping up in the back of my mind: *surrender*.

We don't always love that word, do we? I'll be the first to admit that it often makes me think of weakness, of giving up, of relinquishing my (imagined) rights. The reality, however, is that when we walk with the Lord, a surrendered life is actually our highest aim. It's what we're after! It's not necessarily what we think we want on the days when we think we've mapped out a really good plan.

So here's what we remind ourselves: *No matter what, the Lord's plan is better.*

No matter what.

It's so easy to forget, but those "frustrating interruptions" just might be divine appointments. That's why it's good to set aside the whining and the "why-ing" and focus on the "what."

- Lord, what would you have me learn from this unexpected shift in plans?
- Lord, what is the best way I can serve and love in this situation?
- Lord, what are the places in my life where I'm tempted to elevate my plans above Yours?

As we surrender to the Lord's agenda and not our own—as we thoughtfully and prayerfully respond to our circumstances instead of merely reacting—we inevitably discover that the Lord will not leave us permanently frustrated. He is always up to something new, so we can trust that those unexpected, unscheduled interruptions are invitations to cooperate with Him, to join Him in His work here on earth. He is making all things new (Revelation 21:5), and although the timetable for that certainly isn't up to us, it is *absolutely* a gift to know that He's at work in our lives. Since He's never going to leave us as He finds us, He is constantly teaching us. And sometimes what seems super inconvenient—whether it's an interruption in our own lives or the life of someone we care about—is valuable instruction from the heart of our Father.

Let's surrender to the lesson.

READ ISAIAH 45:1-13.

1. Can you think of a recent interruption or inconvenience that really got on your nerves? Maybe a time when you felt that your plans were pretty awesome and, for whatever reason, they didn't happen?

2. When you look back on that time, can you think of something the Lord might have been trying to show you? Do you think there's a way you could have responded differently?

_____

_____

3. Is surrender difficult for you? Explain.

_____

_____

_____

4. Look again at Isaiah 45:9–10. How do we "argue" with the Lord, even if we don't necessarily say anything?

_____

_____

Today's Prayer

_____

_____

_____

_____

_____

_____

_____

_____

_____

_____

_____

Day 56

*T*he culture we live in is persistent.

We don't always realize it, because we're so inundated with screens and apps and shows that most of us live with an omnipresent buzz of daily news, news feeds, and notifications. Half the time we might not even be able to pinpoint what we're hearing. But if you watch television, listen to music, or glance at social media for longer than about ten minutes—and if you pay attention—you'll start to pick up on certain messages being broadcast over and over again.

For example:

- You need to be award-worthy talented in at least one area.
- You need to be famous because clearly fame is awesome.
- You need to be hot.
- You need an obscene amount of money to live the life you want.
- You need the world's approval.

I'll cut to the chase and tell you that all of those messages are super annoying to me.

I'll even go one step further: I think that if Jesus were sitting with you right now, He'd tell you that those messages are super annoying to Him too.

Because if you belong to Christ, you can rest in the peace of knowing that culture is not the boss of you. You only have to look at Scripture to remember that the Lord's message is much different from much of what you'll see when you're scrolling through social media or flipping through channels—and it's also infinitely more liberating.

For example:

- You are uniquely gifted and empowered by the Holy Spirit. (1 Corinthians 12:11)
- You are here on this earth to make God famous. (Psalm 105:1)
- You are called to be holy. (1 Peter 1:15)
- You are confident that your real treasure is in heaven. (Matthew 6:19–21)

- You are seeking God's approval, not man's. (Galatians 1:10)

Granted, God's standard is, you know, a *smidge* higher than what the world dangles in front of us, but what we so often forget is that there is peace when we make Him our first priority. There is rest. There is a quiet confidence that keeps us going when times are hard. There is deep assurance that grounds us when circumstances feel crazy. There is grace that grows in our weakness. And He is the Source and the Giver of every single one of those things.

Yes, it's tempting to buy into what the culture tells us. It's tempting to want the looks and the money and the guy and the recognition and the big pat on the back. It's tempting to think that if we can just check off all those items on our imaginary scorecard, we'll be good and life will be awesome. But deep down—whether we like to admit it or not—chasing the superficial can never satisfy.

So, in the middle of all the racket, let's make sure to tune our ear to our heavenly Father. His voice is the only one that can truly promise all we need—joy, hope, and peace. Listen up.

READ 1 JOHN 2:15–17.

1. Is there any topic you run across on social media (or in the news) that makes you feel like you're not measuring up in some way?

2. What are some practical ways you can "hear" (not literally, but as you read Scripture and pay attention to the promptings of the Holy Spirit) the Lord's voice more clearly?

3. Can you identify anything you're chasing, so to speak, even though you know that thing has no eternal value?

_____

_____

_____

4. Are there any ways you let the culture boss you around?

_____

_____

_____

_____

Today's Prayer

_____

_____

_____

_____

_____

_____

_____

_____

_____

_____

_____

_____

_____

Day 51

So one time, when I was young and foolish, I went somewhere I shouldn't have with someone I shouldn't have been with. (Got all that?) I also stayed way too long. This was back before everyone walked around with a cell phone in his or her pocket, so when my conscience started to sting a little bit and I decided it would be best if I let my parents know where I was, I found a landline phone. I dialed my parents' number, and I will never forget hearing the sound of my daddy's voice on the other end. I mean, I liked to think I was grown and rational and Miss Independent, but I wasn't so grown that my daddy couldn't inspire a little fear and trembling.

I stuttered out the details of where I was and who was with me, and finally Daddy spoke: "Don't you think you need to come home?"

"Daddy," I replied, "it's fine. We're not doing anything wrong." It wasn't my finest hour in terms of accepting responsibility, especially since I wasn't supposed to be there in the first place. But to his credit, Daddy didn't lose his ever-livin' mind. Instead, he said, "You know, I think you need to come on home. It doesn't look good for you to be there, and I don't think you're setting a great example for younger girls who might look up to you."

"Oh, they don't know I'm here," I answered. And yes, I was totally missing the point. That's because deep down I was so blasé about the whole thing that I probably shook my hair and applied a fresh coat of mascara when I said it.

"You need to come on home," Daddy said. "You don't have any business there. So come home."

I could hear the edge in his voice, so I did what he asked and went home. But I remember driving down the highway and thinking that he was being so old-fashioned. I wasn't doing anything to get in any trouble and really, why was being at that person's house even a big deal? PARENTS ARE SO OVERPROTECTIVE.

No doubt that was just the tip of my disobedient iceberg, but it was years before I saw that particular incident through a different lens. When

I finally did (and it was probably ten or fifteen years later), it was like one aha moment after another.

Here. I will share a few of them:

1. My daddy loved the Lord and loved me. He was my covering, and every single time I disobeyed and stepped out from under his covering, I put myself at risk.

2. I should have absolutely been mindful of how younger girls might view my actions. There's great responsibility that accompanies influence in someone's life.

3. Consistent disobedience in the little things is like dress rehearsal for disobeying in bigger and more serious ways. The more you practice, the better you get.

4. Daddy was one hundred percent right. I was one hundred percent wrong.

5. I disregarded my earthly father just like I can be tempted to disregard my heavenly Father. Daddy's rules weren't dumb. My insistence on making my own rules, however . . . well, *that* was dumb.

We all like to think we know best. But we'll never know best until we're willing to submit to loving authority (sometimes that's in the form of a parent, sometimes a mentor, and sometimes Scripture). What a gift to be loved when we're stubborn or slow to learn a lesson. Thank the Lord for loving, gracious authority today. It is such a gift!

READ EPHESIANS 6:1–4.

1. Can you think of a time when you've known an authority figure was right but you insisted on defying him or her? How'd that work out for you?

2. Is willful rebellion an issue in your life? Or do you tend to be more of a rule follower?

3. What do our relationships with authorities on earth often reveal to us about the state of our hearts? What do they show us about our relationship with our Father in heaven?

4. Read Proverbs 29:23. Write, doodle, or illustrate it here.

Today's Prayer

Day 58

*E*very once in a while, someone will ask me what I dreamed of doing when I was younger. And without fail, my immediate inclination is to respond with this answer:

"Oh, I didn't have any dreams."

I realize it may sound a little harsh (and maybe sad?), but as best I can recall, it's the truth. For the most part I have always been deeply practical, way more concerned with what's realistic than with something I might consider a pie-in-the-sky possibility. Given that, I probably discounted and dismissed anything that might qualify as a dream for the future long before that thing ever had an opportunity to take root in my heart.

As I've gotten older, though, I've grown to appreciate that our dreams for the future can actually propel us forward in our callings. I've come to realize that many times it's the Lord who puts those dreams on our hearts. After all, if we don't dream a little bit about what *could* be, we run the risk of living without vision. Plus, praying about those dreams and following the Lord as He leads us through them—well, that's an adventure of a lifetime right there.

(Keep in mind that I never, ever thought I'd write a book, so I know firsthand about the joy that comes from following God into the unexpected.)

(And it is such a blast. Thank you and amen.)

All that to say: even though there's a time and a place for practicality, there's also a time and a place to dream big dreams with God. So if you're pondering the passions and desires He has planted in your heart and maybe dreaming a little bit about how those things might play out in the future, consider these questions when you pray:

1. If your dream comes to fruition, will God be glorified?
2. Will pursuing your dream require you to abandon your integrity in any way?

3. Is there anything in your present-day life—behavior, habits, sin—that could leave you with regrets and compromise your dream down the road?
4. Do your parents, mentors, and other leaders in your life agree this path is a wise and healthy one for you?
5. Are you doing the practical things in the here and now that will help you in the future?

If there's a downside to being a dreamer, I guess it's the possibility that dreams can become idols, and that we can get so preoccupied with a dream we miss the blessings in our real, right now life. We also run the risk of failure, but as theologian William G. T. Shedd once said, "A ship is safe in harbor, but that's not what ships are for." So whatever your dreams happen to be, remember this: somebody has to have that job or raise those kids or make that music or serve the lonely or fly airplanes—so why not you?

Tell God your dreams. Ask Him to guide and direct your steps, keeping you in the center of His will. He will do it.

Dream on, my friend.

READ PROVERBS 16:1–9.

1. Do you have any big dreams for your future? What are a few of them?

2. When you think about your dreams, do they seem realistic or unrealistic to you? Why do you think you have that reaction?

3. Have you ever had a dream come true and then the reality of it was nothing like you expected? What did you learn from that?

4. Reread the five questions in today's devotion. Does anything jump out at you? Are you on the right course, do you think?

Today's Prayer

Day 59

*Y*ou know how sometimes the oddest things can send you from zero to ten on the White-Hot Fireball of Fury scale? Those times when you're perfectly fine and maybe even humming your favorite song and then suddenly a bolt of anger rises up from the bottom of your feet to the top of your head and *justice will be yours*? In all honesty, it can be difficult to remember what Jesus would do in those moments.

Because, I'm sorry, the person who's in front of you at the grocery store with fourteen items in the ten-items-or-less line? *May the Lord have mercy on her soul.*

Or someone is driving twenty miles below the speed limit in the passing lane on the interstate? *We can only trust that God will hold that person accountable.*

I mean, what is it with all of our big feelings and big confrontations and big reactions? If someone professes Jesus as Lord of her life, then why is she stirring up drama with her friends? Why would someone leave mean-spirited comments on social media? Why is a person so fired-up angry over being cut off in traffic that she'd roll down her window and scream some words that she certainly wouldn't repeat in church?

I promise that I'm not being idealistic about this. I believe I've already expressed my own personal issues with people who ignore the guidelines for using the express lane. I just feel like maybe our collective fuse has gotten a little short, and as a result it doesn't take a whole lot to set us off.

So how do we handle our anger without hurting someone else? How, in the heat of the moment, do we remind ourselves that "human anger does not accomplish God's righteousness" (James 1:20)?

Here are three quick reminders that might help:

1. **Ask the Lord for humility.** *"He leads the humble in what is right and teaches them his way" (Psalm 25:9).* So many times my anger is a by-product of an inflated sense of self. That leads to thinking that if I am being inconvenienced, the person causing that

inconvenience needs to face a consequence of my own making. However, I'm going to react poorly if I'm operating out of pride.

2. **Ask the Lord for patience.** *"Don't let your spirit rush to be angry, for anger abides in the heart of fools" (Ecclesiastes 7:9).* I know this is a newsflash to some of us, but everything doesn't have to happen on our own personal timetables. Often our impulsiveness—our unwillingness to be delayed or to listen or to just understand that sometimes people have bad days—causes us to act in ways we regret. Waiting even thirty seconds to react can often make a tough situation so much better.

3. **Ask the Lord for gentleness.** *"A gentle answers turns away anger, but a harsh word stirs up wrath" (Proverbs 15:1).* Just because we feel angry doesn't mean we have to act or speak out of that anger. We can often diffuse a tense situation by intentionally practicing gentleness when we might not necessarily *feel* like being gentle. I've also found that responding with gentleness calms *me* down; it's the gift that keeps on giving.

And listen. I know. None of these options are nearly as dramatic as honking your horn for upwards of twenty seconds and then screaming, "MOVE IT, GRANDMA" as you whip around the slow car in the passing lane.

I'm pretty sure, though, that Jesus would be on board with our humility, our patience, and our gentleness. Let's honor Him with how we respond in tense situations today.

READ PSALM 37:8-9.

1. How would you characterize your temper? Even-keeled? Long fuse? Short fuse? What leads you to think that about yourself?

2. Have you ever lost your temper in sort of a spectacular fashion? What were the circumstances? How did you feel afterward?

_____

_____

3. Is there anything that consistently sets you off in terms of your temper? Any issue or situation that tends to put you on edge? Any people who experience the brunt of your temper more than others? Reflect on that a bit.

_____

_____

4. Look up Proverbs 29:11. Write, doodle, or illustrate it here.

_____

_____

Today's Prayer

_____

_____

_____

_____

_____

_____

_____

_____

_____

_____

Day 60

*T*onight has been a totally average night at our house. I mean, I know this probably sounds super glamorous, but I made homemade pizza for supper, we cleaned up the kitchen, I answered a few emails, and currently Hazel the dog and I are snuggled up on the guest room bed so that I can do some writing while I simultaneously watch a football game. My husband has fallen asleep in his recliner *(#40sAreCrazy)*, and Alex is watching a TV show on my iPad. We're not doing anything special, we're not in the middle of a meaningful family activity, and we might even be prioritizing our relaxation more than usual considering that it's a weeknight.

BUT OH MY GOODNESS. A few minutes ago I stopped typing and just sat here for a few minutes on this non-eventful night when we certainly wouldn't win any prizes for adventure or excitement. I know it sounds strange, but I felt overwhelmed with gratitude and contentment. On the surface I totally get that it might seem like we're so boring that you kind of want to cry, but I promise, there is so much to be thankful for right here in the middle of the mundane.

- We're together.
- We love each other, even when we drive each other crazy.
- We love being home.
- There is peace in this house.
- I was in my pajamas by five o'clock this afternoon.
- When I'm home, I feel total freedom to be my nerdiest, goofiest self. This is such a gift.
- We're committed to each other. We're committed to this family.
- The Lord really is our joy, our hope, and our strength.
- It rained twice this week.
- We love to laugh together.
- My husband and I have known each other since we were children, and we still haven't run out of things to talk about.
- This stage of motherhood is my favorite so far.

- I get to write books. I don't think I'll ever get over that.
- There's a container of Trader Joe's Dark Chocolate Peanut Butter Cups in the kitchen. In case of emergency, you understand.

And here's why I mention all of that.

It's so easy to get caught in a pattern of being grateful for the big things. Of course it's good to be grateful, period, and there are times when it's flat-out easier to be grateful because so many fantastic things are happening.

But here's what I challenge you to do: Today—which might be ordinary, might be spectacular, or might be terrible (I hope not, though), go somewhere and sit by yourself for fifteen or twenty minutes. Take your journal. And take that time to actively practice gratitude. Make a list. Remind yourself how the Lord is providing for you in different areas of your life. And as best you can, try to think about the everyday gifts that you might be tempted to take for granted. Maybe it's the fact that you ran into a friend on the way to class, or maybe you unexpectedly had time to meet your mom for lunch, or maybe the clouds parted and the angels sang and you actually managed to take a nap this afternoon.

Sometimes we think we'll finally be content when we have everything we want, but true contentment comes when we're grateful for what we already have. The Lord loves you so much. Thank Him for His good gifts today.

READ PHILIPPIANS 4:11-12.

1. Does gratitude come naturally to you?

2. What's a situation where you've been especially grateful lately? Maybe the restoration of a relationship? Or an answer to a specific prayer? Or a way that the Lord has provided?

3. Are you generally a content person? Or do you typically have a "want to or need to" list in the back of your head? Explain.

4. You know that gratitude list I suggested you write in your journal? Did anything you listed take you by surprise? Was there anything small or seemingly unimportant that you realized you're really grateful for?

Today's Prayer

Day 61

*I*t was probably way back in Vacation Bible School when I first learned Mark 12:30: "Love the Lord your God with all your heart, with all your soul, with all your mind, and with all your strength." If I had to guess I'd say we probably did some motions to help us memorize the verse, and then, more than likely, I ran off and played Ping-Pong or Four Square.

I believe the term you're looking for is "impressive spiritual depth."

As an adult I've continued to hear this verse, and inevitably, as I mentally break it apart, here's where I land:

- **"with all my heart"**—Jesus Christ is my heartbeat; I care and I love others because He first loved me.
- **"with all my soul"**—My spirit longs to be free in Him; my whole being longs to glorify Him.
- **"with all my mind"**—Ummm, this is a little trickier.
- **"with all my strength"**—By the Lord's grace, I will diligently and consistently use the life I've been given to make Him known.

Why is the mind such a struggle? I mean, what is that, y'all? Scripture says for us to "be renewed in the spirit of your minds" (Ephesians 4:23) and to "be transformed by the renewing of your mind" (Romans 12:2), so clearly the mind is key in the life of a Christian. But when the mind is also the dwelling place for doubts, cynicism, unbelief, anxiety, fear, impure thoughts, shame, and resentments, just to name a few, it can be quite a battleground.

So that begs the question: how do we fight the good fight when it comes to loving God with our minds? I don't have an exact formula or an exhaustive list, but we definitely can "armor up" in the following ways:

1. **Consistent study of Scripture.** It's difficult to love someone we don't know, and the Bible is where we get to know God. If we want to love Him with our minds, we have to figure out who He is and what He's about.

2. **Intentional time in prayer.** We surrender our minds to the Lord when we pray. We adore Him. We praise Him. We also confess the stuff in our minds that separates us from Him.

3. **Scripture memorization.** When we hide God's Word in our hearts (Psalm 119:11), we're also hiding it in our minds. This enables us to think about the Lord from the correct perspective, and it also alters *how* we think so that it's in a way that honors Him. His Word becomes the filter through which we make our decisions.

4. **Wisdom about what we see, read, and hear.** We give the enemy mental ground when we watch, read, and listen to things that feed our flesh and infiltrate our minds with lies and impure thoughts. Be wise. It is difficult to love the Lord with our minds when our minds are entangled in sin.

5. **Actively remembering His character and His attributes.** This doesn't have to be anything formal. But you know how sometimes you think about someone you love, and you smile, and you start to think about all the reasons you love that person? We can do that for God too. Think about who He is and all He has done. Use your mind to glorify Him.

Love Him well today.

READ MARK 12:28-34.

1. Does your thought life ever get in the way of your faith? Explain.

_____

_____

2. When you think about the character of God, what are the first three attributes that come to mind?

_____

3. When you think about loving God with your heart, soul, mind, and strength, which one of those happens the most naturally for you? Why do you think that is?

_____

_____

4. Look up Colossians 3:2. Write it down in a place where you will see it every single day.

_____

_____

Today's Prayer

_____

_____

_____

_____

_____

_____

_____

_____

_____

_____

_____

_____

Day 62

As I write this, the state of Alabama is in the middle of a drought. We haven't had rain in over a month—and we didn't have much the month before that—so everything here is uncharacteristically dry and dusty. The pond behind our house looks like it's half as big as it was three or four weeks ago, and whenever people mow their grass or use a leaf blower, it creates a haze of dirt that seems to take forever to settle. The grass crunches underneath our feet when we walk across the backyard, and the trees look gray and lifeless. Everywhere we go, people are sneezing and coughing; we're just not used to living in these conditions.

It's occurred to me more than once that right now the outdoors looks a whole lot like my heart sometimes feels. Just as the ground gets dry and brittle without the water that nourishes it, so does my heart. And while the ground, more than anything else, needs a good rainstorm, my heart, more than anything else, is in continual need of Living Water. After all, that's what Jesus says He gives (John 7:38), and my heart is in continual need of Jesus.

I imagine that many of us have walked through times with the Lord when it seemed as if our hearts were filled to overflowing. But there have also, no doubt, been other instances when our hearts were as dry as the desert. That less-than desirable transformation can happen for all sorts of reasons: it might be because we've distanced ourselves from church, because we're battling some habitual sin, because the troubles of the world have overwhelmed us, or because of our imagined self-sufficiency like we see the Lord address in Jeremiah 2:13: "For my people have . . . abandoned me, the fountain of living water, and dug cisterns for themselves—cracked cisterns that cannot hold water."

Sometimes we may feel as if we're the only person who's struggling, but it's not uncommon for believers to experience a trek through what feels like a spiritual desert. Still, when we're wandering, so to speak, it's wise to sit down with a trusted leader or friend and consider the *why*:

- Am I somehow feeling worn down by my circumstances—things like relationship struggles, school or work stresses, health issues, or family tensions?
- Am I chasing after idols?
- Have I intentionally or unintentionally tried to put some distance between the Lord and me?
- Have I intentionally or unintentionally tried to put some distance between my Christian friends and me?
- Have I somehow lost sight of His majesty, His power, and His deep love for His children?

If there are parched places in your life that need ministry and healing, pursue that. Remember that by God's grace, we don't have to sit around and wait for a storm to hit. Our Living Water is an ever-flowing fountain, which means we simply have to connect to the Source. Isaiah 44:3 says, "For I will pour water on the thirsty land, and streams on the dry ground." In John 7:37, Jesus "stood up and cried out, 'If anyone is thirsty, let him come to me and drink.'"

He pours out everything we need. He waters the dry land of our hearts. All praise to the Living Water, the Giver of life.

READ ISAIAH 41:17–20.

1. Has there ever been a time when you went through some sort of spiritual desert? Explain.

_____

_____

_____

_____

_____

2. When things are off-kilter in your spiritual life, how does that affect the rest of your life?

_____

_____

3. What does water do for us? Why is it such a perfect metaphor for Jesus? What does Living Water supply?

_____

_____

4. Chris Tomlin wrote a song called "All My Fountains." Look it up and write the chorus here.

_____

_____

Today's Prayer

_____

_____

_____

_____

_____

_____

_____

_____

_____

_____

_____

Day 63

So what I'm about to say isn't at all lighthearted, but it's important. Critical, even.

Salvation isn't simply "asking Jesus into your heart" so that you avoid spending eternity in hell. Salvation isn't the result of bowing your head or walking an aisle or praying a prayer. Salvation is embracing, by faith, two realities: (1) the hopelessly sinful state of your own heart, and (2) the hope of a Savior who paid the penalty for your sins on the cross, overcame death, and ascended to heaven, where He continually intercedes for you and where you will eventually enjoy eternity with Him.

There's nothing anyone can do to earn salvation; it is a free gift of grace. Jesus came so that you "may have life and have it in abundance" (John 10:10). Life with Him really is abundant; salvation through Jesus Christ transforms you from the inside out, reorders your priorities, and changes how you live.

In the simplest terms, we could say that salvation makes you different.

But as you know, different isn't always easy.

Different means that in situations where others might back away or compromise, you stand up for what's right. You stand up for Truth. You stand up for people, the image-bearers of God. You stand up for the gospel.

Being different because you belong to Jesus changes how you respond to situations in your day-to-day life. How could it not? Sometimes that means you sacrifice your money; sometimes it means you sacrifice your time. It almost always means that you sacrifice your pride. And one approach to ministry that can be particularly impactful is when you don't just look at the world around you . . . you take time to *see*.

And oh, y'all, there is so much to see.

- the person crying in the hall between classes
- the kid who's disrespectful to authority but clearly hurting inside
- the elderly neighbor whose husband just passed away
- the drugstore checkout clerk who seems unusually stressed

- the sibling frustrated by struggles with schoolwork
- the outgoing classmate who feels like no one really knows her
- the teacher weary from family demands and late-night grading
- the family who has recently added two foster children to their household
- the visitor at church who looks like she doesn't know a soul

And that's just scratching the surface of the situations we can find in our own backyard, so to speak. We are surrounded on all sides by brokenness and heartache and the accompanying needs, so we have opportunity after opportunity to shine some light on dark or difficult places.

It's good to remember that you don't do these things because you're trying to build a reputation for yourself, and you can't save the world, of course. But because Jesus Christ has saved you—because He has called you by name and made you His—you are His ambassador on earth. You get to share His peace, His mercy, and His love with other people.

Salvation makes you different to make a difference.

What a calling, what a responsibility, and what a privilege. Praise the Lord.

READ ROMANS 1:16–17.

1. Was there ever a time when you didn't necessarily understand what it meant to be saved? Or when you thought it was something you had to earn?

_____

_____

2. How has salvation made you different?

_____

_____

3. Are there any situations or circumstances in your life that you used to look at but now you can really see? Here's an example: maybe you thought a relative was aloof and standoffish, but now you can see and understand that he or she is disillusioned by disappointments?

_____

_____

4. Look up Romans 5:8. Write, illustrate, or doodle it here.

_____

_____

_____

Today's Prayer

_____

_____

_____

_____

_____

_____

_____

_____

_____

_____

_____

_____

_____

_____

Day 64

A few weeks ago my sister-in-law sent me the most gorgeous orchid for my birthday. The florist delivered it to my work, and after I spent a couple of days with those off-white blooms decorating the corner of my desk, I decided that I didn't want to take the orchid to my house; it added way too much cheer to the workday. Plus, I have a little bit of a black thumb (I have yet to meet a plant I can't kill in record time), so the fact that the orchid seemed to be thriving was an unexpected bonus.

And about ten days later, the craziest thing happened: that orchid started blooming like crazy. I couldn't wrap my brain around it, and I totally did that obnoxious thing that people sometimes do when they meet with the tiniest bit of success. I started acting like I knew all the orchid-growing secrets.

- "Oh, yeah, you know, you just water it once a week."
- "Well, what I've found is that orchids really respond best if they're in indirect sunlight."
- "I chose that spot on my desk for it because I thought it would really respond to the cool air from the AC vent."

TOTAL PRETENDER.

But here's the real kicker. That orchid has continued to bloom like that's its job (which, I don't know, maybe that *is* an orchid's job). It's stunning. People walk into my office and see that orchid and start singing hymns and spiritual songs (okay, not really that last thing). And a couple of days ago, two senior girls popped by between classes, and as they reached to grab some candy from my candy bowl, one of them said, "Mrs. Hudson! That orchid is so pretty!"

"I know!" I replied. And before I could launch into my explanation of all the ways I had nurtured the orchid since it had come into my care, the other senior girl piped up: "Hey, did you know that it can take them six years to bloom?"

"Really?" her friend answered.

"Yep," she said. "That's a long time."

Sure enough, I consulted the Google, and it takes orchids a sweet forever to bloom, some as long as ten years. I looked at that stunning plant on the corner of my desk, and I thought about the length of time it had taken to produce its blooms. I couldn't get over the parallels to how the Lord works in our lives.

Because sometimes there's stuff we think we want with all our hearts—maybe even things we believe the Lord is asking us to do—and for whatever reason, they're just not happening. We pray, we fast, and we wait, but our circumstances never change.

Don't be discouraged. Continue in hope. If those areas of your life are designed to bloom, they most certainly will—in God's time. And who knows? There might be some other part of your life that bursts into bloom when you're not even expecting it.

No matter where or how it happens, it will be beautiful. Pray for grace to trust Him more—no matter the outcome.

READ ECCLESIASTES 3:1-8.

1. How well do you handle waiting? Are you patient, or does it drive you a little bit crazy?

_____

_____

_____

2. Is there any area of your life where you feel like you've been waiting on the Lord for a long time?

_____

_____

_____

3. When you think about your future, what would you like to see bloom? A certain gift or talent? Family? Career? Ministry opportunities? Be as specific or as general as you'd like.

_____

_____

4. Look up Psalm 27:14. Read it out loud, and then write it here.

_____

_____

_____

Today's Prayer

_____

_____

_____

_____

_____

_____

_____

_____

_____

_____

_____

Day 65

*O*ver the last year or so I've started sending a lot of voice texts because, well, some of my mom friends got me hooked on it. We talk back and forth every single day via Voxer, which reminds me: yay for communicating without having to find letters on a tiny keyboard! You'll understand exactly what I mean in about twenty years when your eyes decide they're no longer interested in helping you see things like words.

Well. Not too long ago a friend and I were messaging back and forth, and both of us clearly were dealing with what I like to call "ish-ahs" (that's Southern for *issues*). My friend was wrestling with health stuff, and I was at high tide with grief. Honestly, I'd missed Mama so much the previous couple of days that I felt like I would never get to the bottom of all the sad, and my friend was pretty discouraged by how awful she'd been feeling. So we relayed all the details of what we were working through, and within about five minutes of sharing the nitty gritty, hey-life-is-hard-sometimes details, I sent my friend another message about how really, I had so much to be thankful for, and I was sure everything would be fine.

And then she sent me a message that she was super hopeful that her medicine would kick in soon, and no doubt it was all going to be great because she had a fun family trip coming up that weekend, and she couldn't wait to feel better for it.

No joke. Within ten minutes we went from some gut-level fear and sadness to confident assurance that better days were ahead.

It was a total 180 in terms of our perspective, and for sure that 180 was possible because we know the Lord and we've learned that we can trust Him with the hard stuff. But . . . that conversation with my friend reminded me of something I think is worth mentioning: when we're walking through difficulty, we can be tempted to upsell it. Sometimes circumstances are challenging and heart-wrenching and anxiety-inducing, and in those moments we don't have to pretend like, *Everything's fine! I'm doing great! I don't even have time to panic or cry because I'm just so busy feeling awesome about everything!*

I'm not saying that we should be doom and gloom. I mean, my goodness, we do have big-time Hope. In fact, our darkest moments are often when the Light seems brightest. That being said, God isn't deterred by our honest reactions. He isn't taken aback when we vent to a friend. We can be vulnerable and real—without feeling pressure to spin the details to make them cheerier than they actually are—while still being utterly mindful of God's faithfulness.

Life can be tough. That's a given. And God can handle the times when we need to sit in our sadness and disappointments for a little while. He doesn't ask us to work it all out, get it all together, and *then* tell our people what's going on. He tells us to bear one another's burdens, to live real life together, and to trust Him to work in and through every bit of it.

There's no need to constantly upsell or spin. But oh what grace it is to walk through hardships with loving friends, to be completely honest about our feelings and questions, and to know a gracious God who lovingly reorients our perspective as He reminds us of the Source of our hope.

There's no "ish-ah" that's too big for Him.

READ 1 JOHN 3:16–24.

1. Can you think of a time when you've downplayed a significant problem—or tried to "upsell" a difficulty, as if it's really not a big deal?

2. Even if you don't have personal experience with question 1, play psychologist for a minute: Why do we do that? Why do we seem to feel like we need to discount or dismiss the fact that sometimes our circumstances are just flat-out tough?

3. Is there any issue (ish-ah!) in your life right now that you're tempted to pretend is better than it actually is?

4. Who's a person who makes it easy for you to get gut-level honest about life? What makes you feel safe with her (or him)?

Today's Prayer

Day 66

*A*fter a year of vowing that I didn't know why anybody needed one, I recently got a FitBit. Little did I know that it would take approximately four-ish hours for me to become completely dialed in to all the FitBit features. Suddenly I could check my heart rate, I could see how many steps I'd taken, I could find out how many calories I'd burned, and if I wore the FitBit when I slept, I could analyze my sleeping habits. It's been an onslaught of daily information I didn't even know I wanted, and I am surprisingly crazy about the turquoise band that is continually wrapped around my wrist. In a weird way, it's almost like an ever-present accountability partner.

Well. Yesterday I was looking at my FitBit app to see how well I'd slept the night before (answer: not very) when the strangest thought occurred to me: wouldn't it be awesome if we had some variation of a FitBit for our relationships with the Lord? I don't know—maybe we'd call it a Heavenly Helper (H^2 for short)—and after wearing it all day (maybe around our heads like a halo because YES), we'd open the app before bed to see how well we followed Jesus during our waking hours. Can you even imagine?

- You were 67 percent holy today.
- Your thoughts were pure for 4 hours and 32 minutes.
- You fought temptation 72 times. Good job!

On one hand, it might be nice to have an objective assessment of how we're walking out our faith. But the reality, of course, is that it would never work because we'd get awfully self-righteous if those numbers got high enough—or we'd be completely discouraged that we weren't seeing the results we'd hoped for.

Faith was never meant to be a checklist.

By God's design, there's not a single one of us who can overcome our sinfulness on our own. If we could, we'd have no need for a Savior—we'd just BRING IT with the holy awesome every single day. So if we want to continue growing in love and compassion and godliness, we really only have one surefire method (and no, it isn't our sassy H² halo).

We have to abide.

The word *abide* is translated from the Greek word *menó*, which means "to stay, continue, dwell, endure, be present, remain, stand, tarry (for)."[4] We stay with Him, and He stays with us. The Bible gives us the image of a vine and branches and reminds us that we cannot bear fruit apart from Him; we must be constantly connected (John 15:1–17). This can only happen through study of the Word and the power of the Holy Spirit. You and I can do a lot, but we can't generate holiness (or bear fruit, for that matter). To put it in modern terminology, Jesus is our ride or die. He is our constant Companion, our Counselor, and our Savior King.

We might not be able to wear Him on our wrists, but He's in our hearts and leading us exactly where we want and need to be.

READ JOHN 15:1–11.

1. Do you ever have a "scorecard" mentality about your faith? Maybe you want to follow all the rules and get some gold stars? Why is that such a comfortable place for many of us?

   _____

   _____

2. Has there ever been a time in your life when you battled self-righteousness? Or maybe a time when you've been on the receiving end of someone else's moral superiority? What was that like?

   _____

   _____

---

4. "Menó" *Blue Letter Bible*, accessed March 10, 2017, https://www.blueletterbible.org/lang/lexicon/lexicon.cfm?Strongs=G3306&t=ESV.

3. According to John 15:5, what can you do apart from Jesus?

_____

_____

_____

4. When you think of an earthly life that bears great fruit, what person comes to mind? Why? Do you see evidence that he or she has abided in Jesus?

_____

_____

_____

Today's Prayer

_____

_____

_____

_____

_____

_____

_____

_____

_____

_____

_____

_____

_____

Day 67

$\mathcal{S}$ometimes we can dream about something for a long time, and then, when we finally get our shot, it doesn't work out anything like we expected it to.

Several years ago my son couldn't wait to play tackle football for the first time. He was fired up at the first practice, hoping to catch on quickly, knowing full well that there was a great big learning curve ahead.

After a few weeks, Alex had gotten used to the drills and was really enjoying his teammates. He was thrilled to have a number and a spot on the roster. And then right before the first game, he found out that, because of his age, he was actually supposed to be on a different team. He had the option to switch to a new team—where he wouldn't know many people but might get to play in games—or stay on his original team without being able to compete since he was past the age limit.

"I'm staying with my team," Alex said. For the rest of the season, he continued to go to every practice, but he never played a down in an actual game. His coach asked him if he'd like to be the water boy during the games, and week after week, that's exactly what he did. He practiced three days a week, and during the games, he handed out water.

It was nothing like what he expected or wanted. But his daddy and I remain convinced that in the big picture of Alex's life and character, that particular football season will continue to be so important. Our boy learned about loyalty, commitment, service, and humility—all more valuable than blocking a defensive lineman or recovering a fumble. And even though he may not have realized it, he learned firsthand about characteristics that matter a great deal to God.

Here's the thing: *when it comes to humility, the Lord's ways run contrary to the world's ways.* Truthfully, His ways seem upside down. For example, Scripture tells us that the first will be last and the last will be first (Matthew 19:30). It says that whoever saves his life will lose it, but whoever loses his life will find it (Mark 9:35). In 2 Corinthians, Paul tells us that when he is weak, he is strong (12:10).

Every once in a while, we go into situations looking for the lofty. We want to be lifted up, we want to be known, we want attention and adulation and the world's definition of success.

But when the world says "go high," the gospel says, "get low."

That doesn't mean we don't work with all our might at whatever we do. But when no task is beneath us, no act of service is too small, and a high-five from others isn't our motivator, that's when people just might see Jesus in us. Our lives are not our own, and we are not the point. He is.

Don't be discouraged the next time you start a new job, a new season, or a new opportunity and realize that you're going to be behind-the-scenes instead of front-and-center. We'll never learn more about the character of our Savior than when we serve, love, and get low for the glory of God.

READ 2 CORINTHIANS 12:9-10.

1. Has there ever been a time when you were looking forward to being a part of something for a long time and then your role was nothing like you thought it would be? What was that like? (And if not, then how do you think that would make you feel?)

_____

_____

_____

2. Can you think of a time when you had an unexpected opportunity to serve and were blessed by the experience? Explain.

_____

_____

_____

_____

3. Do you have opportunities to serve others on a regular basis? If not, can you think of some ways you could start serving regularly?

4. Read John 3:30. Write, doodle, or illustrate it here.

Today's Prayer

Day 68

*I*t's so easy—and so tempting—to expect that labels will define us.

I'm an Honor Roll student.
I'm vice president of my class.
I'm the fastest runner on my cross-country team.
I'm a trustworthy friend; people tell me their secrets.
I'm the youngest in my family and know how to get what I want.

The problem with labels, though, is that they can't stick forever. They're temporary. You can wear one for a little while, but over time it's going to curl up at the edges. It won't stick as well as it used to. It'll fray and wear and eventually fall off. Even worse, someone might rip it off for you. And after the label is gone, then what?

Who are you then? Well, I'm going to tell you.

You are a deeply loved child of God.
You are fearfully and wonderfully made.
And you are precious in His sight.

It's weird, isn't it? We let all sorts of people (and who knows how many labels) define us. We tell ourselves that our lives will be perfect if we can just get that grade or win this competition or beat that time. We listen to lies and convince ourselves that we're only as good as the number of followers we have on social media, and we hide other people's criticisms in our hearts and play them on repeat when we're alone. We so desperately want to be known *for something* that we'll sometimes settle for being known *for anything*.

And when we do that, we chip away at our true identity, which has only ever been—and will only ever be—in Him. I'm so grateful that Jesus looks at all those other words and labels and names we call ourselves—the things we think will make us known—and lovingly shakes His head.

No, ma'am. Here's what really and truly matters. You are Mine.

Can you remind yourself of that today? You. Are. His. No one else gets to define you. No one else gets to tell you who you are. And because of that, you will never find true and lasting peace in a title, in a role, or in a perfect GPA. You should absolutely do your best at whatever you undertake. (Colossians 3:23 is pretty clear about that "Whatever you do, do it from the heart, as something done for the Lord and not for people" business). But your work—or another person's evaluation of it—has no bearing on your value as a person.

Because in case you've forgotten, I'm happy to remind you: the Lord established and sealed your value before the foundation of time. He created you with great intention. He loves you more than you could ever imagine. And at the end of the day, His opinion is the only one that matters.

So remember:

You are a deeply loved child of God.
You are fearfully and wonderfully made.
And you are precious in His sight.

That's a label worth wearing. And it will never, ever fade.

READ ISAIAH 43:1-9.

1. Are you chasing after any labels? What are they? And if not, what labels have you chased in the past?

2. What problems can arise when we let people or things other than God define us?

3. Do you remember the words to "Jesus Loves Me"? Write them here. Then read them out loud . . . *seriously!*

_____

_____

4. List a few things that have recently reminded you of how much He loves and cares for you.

_____

_____

Today's Prayer

Make a list of prayer requests and praises, or write out whatever's on your heart.

_____

_____

_____

_____

_____

_____

_____

_____

_____

_____

_____

_____

_____

Day 69

*C*urrent culture isn't always supportive or instructive in terms of healthy relationships between young women. In a hundred different ways—both in the media and in the world around us—we're confronted with examples of female friendships marked by selfishness, competition, and pettiness. That's not necessarily real life for most of us, but even still, it's not always easy to know what healthy, life-giving friendship looks like.

We talked a while ago about Mary and Elizabeth, and I actually think we can look to them to teach us a few lessons about what it's like to be part of a healthy friendship.

1. **You are safe.** After Mary heard Gabriel's news, she "hurried" to the home of her cousin and friend Elizabeth (Luke 1:39). If you've ever been through something shocking or unexpected or confusing, you know what a gift it is to be with a friend who just flat-out "gets it"—even if you don't say a word. It's such a relief to know that you can trust someone no matter what. No wonder Mary tried to get to Elizabeth's house quickly.

2. **You are welcomed.** When Mary arrived at Elizabeth's house, Elizabeth didn't ignore Mary or make excuses about how she was six months pregnant and it just wasn't a very good time for company. She immediately welcomed her. That's what real friendship feels like. You are welcome when you are in the other person's company. You aren't an imposition or a source of frustration. You're at ease because you know the other person is for you and on your side.

3. **You are blessed.** Don't get me wrong; I'm not talking about *#blessed*. I'm talking about the fact that a good, true friend will bless you with her words and her actions. She will not try to diminish you or put you down. When Mary arrived at Elizabeth's, Elizabeth immediately knew that Mary was going to be the mother of Jesus. But she wasn't competitive, and she didn't feel like her own pregnancy was somehow less

important. Elizabeth blessed Mary (v. 42) and offered sincere encouragement about the Lord's call on Mary's life.

4. **You are validated.** One of the sweetest things Elizabeth did for Mary was to confirm that Mary was in fact "the mother of my Lord." At a time when her cousin and friend must have felt extremely vulnerable and at least a little uncertain, Elizabeth confirmed what Gabriel said—that Mary was going to be the mother of the Savior of the world—and Elizabeth affirmed Mary's confidence in the Lord's plans for her (v. 45). Elizabeth's reaction and response must have been a giant sigh of relief for Mary.

5. **You are enough.** If you pay attention to Elizabeth's reaction, you'll notice that at no point did Mary try to justify why the Lord had chosen her. I think that's because Elizabeth never doubted Mary's calling. By the same token, Elizabeth didn't feel the need to justify why her pregnancy was important too—because she knew she was enough. There was an absence of neediness and an abundance of grace. That makes for a super-healthy relationship.

Life-giving friendships are a treasure. Pray that the Lord will help you love your friends unconditionally and lavishly today.

READ LUKE 1:46-49.

1. Do you have friends who make you feel safe and welcome? Write a prayer asking the Lord to help you be that kind of friend for someone.

2. When was a time when a friend or family member saw something in you that you didn't see in yourself? Talk about that a little bit.

3. Have you ever been in a situation where a friend confirmed, affirmed, or blessed what the Lord was doing in your life? What were the specifics? How did you respond?

4. In today's Scripture reading Mary demonstrated great joy and confidence in her calling, especially in verse 49. Do you think Elizabeth influenced or affected Mary's perspective? Why or why not?

Today's Prayer

Day 70

*Y*ou know what can be difficult and disillusioning?

When you realize that you're at a place in your life you never wanted to be.

And I'm not talking about a seemingly endless line at Disney World, of course. I'm not even talking about moving to a strange city or facing the harsh reality of re-taking Algebra II in summer school.

I'm talking about finding yourself in the middle of a very real struggle with alcohol. Or feeling trapped in an unhealthy relationship. Or vowing for the umpteenth time to flee from a pornography habit, and then giving in to temptation all over again.

Or maybe you're in a tense stand-off with one of your parents, and neither of you seems willing to give. Maybe there's a secret that has you in its grip to the point that you feel like you'll never be able to shake it.

Those unexpected places—they can be so tough. And discouraging. And also exhausting. But listen to what Jesus says: "Come to me, all of you who are weary and burdened, and I will give you rest" (Matthew 11:28).

I used to read that verse and, in the middle of something difficult, I'd think, *Here I am, so FIX IT, JESUS. I'm ready to rest now!* What I've learned over the years, though, is that while Jesus' words are indeed comforting and full of grace, there's also responsibility on our end of things. He will absolutely take our burden—our bondage to sin—and exchange it for mercy. We, however, have to show up and be willing to do what He asks.

What does that mean? Well, here are some thoughts:

1. **Conviction of sin.** We need to be super clear on one key point: if we're heavy laden because of our sinful decisions, *we've been wrong*. If we're looking for rest from our weariness in sin while still holding on to any notion of our rightness, then on some level we're not willing or ready to surrender.
2. **Willingness to cooperate.** Rest can come in ways that have nothing to do with sleep. Sometimes rest is the peace that

comes with laying down a burden. Sometimes rest is confession. Sometimes rest is placing yourself under someone else's supervision. Pray to be humble and responsive however the Lord leads.

3. **Trusting the Burden Bearer.** No matter how hard or how long the road to restoration and wholeness is, know that the Lord is leading you to a place of peace. Trust that He knows the very best path. We can really complicate a hard situation when we try to hold on to this part of it or manage that part of it. Give Him the whole thing. Trust Him with it. He knows best.

You are braver than you ever imagined.
And you are more loved than you know.

READ 1 CORINTHIANS 10:11-13.

1. Have you or someone you love ever found yourselves in a situation you never planned or wanted? Explain.

_____

_____

_____

_____

2. Are there any personal battles you seem to fight over and over again? Does that battle ever make you feel tired and weary?

_____

_____

_____

_____

3. Why do you think it's so hard for us see our sin for what it is? Why is it so hard to look at it honestly?

4. Are there any areas of your life right now where you know you're in the wrong? List them, and then pray for wisdom.

Today's Prayer

Day 11

$\mathcal{A}$ long time ago (probably before lots of you were even born), I was in a job interview at the place where I still work (spoiler alert: I got the job). The man interviewing me was Dr. K—who remains one of my heroes—and about ten minutes into our conversation, he posed a question I've never forgotten:

> *Mrs. Hudson, self-control is a fruit of the Spirit, and it's essential when it comes to how we communicate with one another here. Do you have a bridled tongue?*

Real talk: I had no idea that "bridled tongue" referred to James 1:26. So I did my best to pick up on the context of the question, and I assumed he was asking me if I could control my reactions, refrain from using harsh words, and resist the urge to gossip. My answer?

I hope so. I think so. I really do try.

So sure, it wasn't my most articulate moment, but I've never forgotten how serious Dr. K was when he asked me that question. It mattered to him. And the older I get, the more I understand why.

For example:

We're living in a very heated political climate. Same for social issues. There's deep division, intense anger, a bottomless well of opinions, and non-stop social media to fuel the fire. Given all of that, there are endless opportunities to take offense, to feel dismissed, to get defensive, and to fire back at a very nice person who was in our fourth-grade class but clearly has lost her mind considering that she now supports *that* candidate or *that* cause. We also have plenty of chances to share our own opinions harshly and without consideration for others.

And somewhere along the line, we've confused having a disagreement with NOW I MUST IMMEDIATELY CONFRONT THIS PERSON. We'd be wise to bridle our tongues so that we don't damage relationships as well as our testimonies. (Really, we need to bridle our fingers considering how heated online comments can be and how prone people are to posting without thinking.) On top of all that, we should be careful about what we repeat. Rumors get passed along as if they're facts, people refuse to consider different perspectives, and civil discourse seems like the exception rather than the rule.

It would be easy to excuse this kind of behavior and say, "Well, that's just how things are now. It is what it is." But as believers, we are called to cool our jets. We're called to simmer down. We're called to be "quick to listen, slow to speak, and slow to anger," and that's not so our interactions with other people will be more polite and kind. It's because "human anger does not accomplish God's righteousness" (James 1:19–20).

Well, then. That's pretty clear, huh?

In James 1:26, we read this: "If anyone thinks he is religious and does not bridle his tongue but deceives his heart, this person's religion is worthless" (ESV). So our "bridled tongue"? Our ability to be self-controlled in terms of what we say and how we say it? It matters so much, y'all.

Pray for wisdom with your words today.

READ JAMES 1:19–26.

1. Does anyone come to mind when you think of someone who is wise in what she says and how she says it? Do you admire those qualities?

_____

_____

_____

2. Besides the fact that Scripture says we need it, what are some practical reasons why it's good to have a bridled tongue?

_____

_____

_____

3. Have you ever been in a situation—either in real life or online—where you said too much, lost your cool, or regretted your words? How did you handle that?

_____

_____

4. When are you most likely to gossip or speak unkindly about someone else?

_____

_____

_____

Today's Prayer

_____

_____

_____

_____

_____

_____

_____

_____

_____

_____

_____

_____

_____

Day 12

Maybe you've heard one of your parents say it. As a parent and a teacher, I've certainly said it way too much. I said it just the other day, in fact.

"I can't give you any more grace."

Nope. Can't do it. No more grace for you.

Now I totally get that there's a practical side to this thing. We associate grace with a pardon. We associate grace with minimized consequences or no consequences at all. As humans we are very imperfect administrators of discipline, and sometimes we reach a point where we think, *That's it. This person isn't learning the lesson. No more grace. Only consequences from here on out.*

But that's not how grace works.

Because when we say, "There's no more grace. I have to draw a hard line with clear consequences," here's what we're forgetting: *there is so much grace in our consequences.* Some of my best, biggest lessons from the Lord have been smack-dab in the middle of tough consequences. And that is pure grace, my friends.

The fact that someone—and Someone—would help us learn and grow as they discipline us? THAT IS SUCH A GOOD THING.

There's no end to grace, y'all. None. We'll never get to the grace finish line. There is always more. Because wherever the Lord is—and, to be clear, He is everywhere—grace abounds. It just might not arrive in the ways we're expecting.

So if you get pulled over and get a speeding ticket? There is grace there. You could have continued to drive fast and been in an accident. Instead, perhaps you will learn to be more attentive when you're on the road. That ticket may discourage you from speeding in the future. It might even be a lesson that a younger friend or sibling needs to see. *Thank you, Lord, for grace.*

So if you feel rejected by a group of girls and don't understand why they're ignoring you? There is grace there. You are discovering what you want and need from friends. You are learning that the people who are rejecting you can't provide that. You will treasure kind, trustworthy friends in the future because you know how much it means to have them. *Thank you, Lord, for grace.*

So if you get caught cheating on a test and have to spend your afternoon in the dean's office? There is grace there. Count your blessings, sister. The jig is up. You did something dishonest, and you're accepting responsibility for it. This could be protection from all manner of dishonesty down the road. You're learning about integrity and why it matters. *Thank you, Lord, for grace.*

No matter where you find yourself, no matter what you do, no matter how far you fall, you can rest assured that grace is waiting on you there.

For every need, for every situation, the Lord's grace is never-ending.

READ JAMES 4:6–10.

1. Do you ever think that grace has an expiration date? Why or why not?

_____

_____

_____

_____

2. What's a situation in which you now realize that tough consequences were oh-so-gracious? Explain.

_____

_____

_____

_____

3. Has there been a certain time in your life that felt like a lesson overload, in a way? Where, by God's grace, you learned one big lesson after another?

_____

_____

4. Read Hebrews 4:16. Write, doodle, or illustrate it here.

_____

_____

_____

Today's Prayer

_____

_____

_____

_____

_____

_____

_____

_____

_____

_____

_____

Day 13

I am a total creature of habit in the mornings. I wake up, take a shower, wrap my hair in a towel, make a cup of coffee, put a breakfast-ish option in the oven, and sit down at the kitchen table for my quiet time while the towel works its magic on my hair and the oven works its magic on the bacon or biscuits or toast. I move through the routine of getting dressed with the same level of predictability. And when Alex and I leave the house for school—typically around 6:45—our first stop is always going to be our neighborhood coffee shop. If I'm going to power through the rest of the morning, then I'm going to need a grande flat white to help me do it.

A week or so ago we left the coffee shop and turned onto the road we normally take to school. We had just come over a hill we travel every day when suddenly we were engulfed by fog. The fog completely clouded the shopping center I would typically be able to see to our left, and if I hadn't memorized our route from driving it so many times, I wouldn't have been able to see our next turn. It was the strangest sensation to be in the middle of what was normally familiar territory, but due to unexpected circumstances, nothing looked like it usually did.

This is exactly where we find ourselves in life sometimes. We're going through our routines, coasting on autopilot, and then something unforeseen happens. It's not a literal fog, but it's for sure a figurative one. And until it lifts, it can seem like it obscures everything you thought you knew to be sure and true. It can certainly leave you wondering which way to go.

So what do you do when the fog hits?

1. **Remember that you need to get your bearings.** Part of growing up is realizing there will be times when you look around and realize your circumstances seem cloudy and confusing. It might be because of difficulty in a relationship or knowing that you have to make a big decision. In those moments, it's okay—and

also wise—to "pull over" for a minute. There is no point trying to move forward when you lack visibility in the here and now.

2. **Remember to look up.** There have been so many times in my life when I couldn't figure out where to go and what to do next. It's so easy to think that we have to make those decisions on our own. But no matter what is going on, the Lord's vision is not obscured. He sees the big picture when we feel like we can't see an inch in front of our face. Pray. Listen. Trust Him.

3. **Remember that things will eventually be clear again.** The fog isn't forever. It will lift. The landscape may look different than you thought, but that's okay. You'll be able to see clearly, and hopefully the change in conditions—along with confidence in the Lord's leading—will bring renewed gratitude and peace.

Remember, the fog is temporary. Clearer skies are ahead.

READ ROMANS 8:18-25.

1. Can you think of a time when you were "coasting along," so to speak, and then life changed in such a way that it felt like a fog had suddenly surrounded you?

_____

_____

2. What tends to be your immediate reaction when you don't know what to do? Frustration? Sadness? Anger? Talk about that for a little bit.

_____

_____

_____

3. Are you typically patient in the waiting? Or are you tempted to keep moving whether you know the right thing to do or not?

_____

_____

_____

4. According to Romans 8:24, what is the hope we cannot see?

_____

_____

_____

_____

Today's Prayer

_____

_____

_____

_____

_____

_____

_____

_____

_____

_____

_____

_____

_____

Day 14

I have some shocking news. You ready?

You are not God.

I KNOW. It's hard to believe, isn't it? DID YOU HAVE ANY IDEA?

And I know I'm being goofy about it, but that's totally on purpose. Because, people, we have a very real tendency to think we can play god in the middle of our everyday circumstances. On any given day, many of us will talk about what situation we're going to fix, what friends we're going to set straight, what behaviors we no longer care for in our leaders, and how, really, we could do all the things so much better and more efficiently if everybody would just listen to us and then follow our wishes.

We may not like to admit it, but from time to time, lots of us secretly (or maybe not-so-secretly) think we could do a fine job of, you know, controlling the whole world—or, at the very least, controlling the part where we live.

So I'll go ahead and be the bad guy so you don't harbor any delusions: You cannot control your future. You cannot control other people. You certainly cannot control the world. And if you could—and I say this in all love—you would be terrible at it. You're not built for it.

You're welcome. I'm just here to encourage.

And seriously.

So many times when we start trying to control different situations, we're not battling arrogance as much as we're battling fear. It's not necessarily that we think we're so awesome and so wise and so capable; lots of times it's just that we're scared. We're scared we're going to get hurt, scared we can't trust God to get us to the other side of that thing (whatever "that thing" happens to be), scared we'll be way too vulnerable if we commit to an honest conversation, or scared we're not going to get what we want. All the unknowns and unknowables put us in a frame of mind where our primary coping mechanism is *Activate Control Mode* ASAP.

But when we're the most tempted to control (and naturally I'm not talking about an actual crisis or emergency, in which case having someone who takes charge is helpful and necessary) is often when we most need to *slow down, pray,* and *wait.* I have learned this the hard way, especially since my personality tends to err on the side of NOW IS WHEN I WILL FIX ALL THE PROBLEMS. Here's the rub, though: our best efforts are futile apart from the wisdom of God. So now, when a situation gets tricky, I abandon my initial instinct to formulate a 29-step to-do list, and instead I pray a very simple prayer:

Lord, I don't understand.
Lord, help me know what to do.

And more often than not, the Lord will redirect me—through His Word, a timely sermon, or the wise counsel of a trusted friend—to service, humility, and compassion.

His ways aren't our ways. And that's a *really* good thing indeed.

READ PSALM 62:5-8.

1. Do you ever think of yourself as being a little bit of a control freak? Why or why not?

_____

_____

_____

_____

2. Can you think of a situation that you really tried to control or manage, and then it didn't turn out anything like you wanted? What was it?

_____

_____

_____

3. Why do you think so many of us are scared of losing control? Do you see any irony in our fear?

_____

_____

_____

4. Write down 1 John 4:8.

_____

_____

_____

_____

Today's Prayer

_____

_____

_____

_____

_____

_____

_____

_____

_____

_____

_____

_____

_____

Day 75

*F*or lots of reasons, this last week has been a big reminder about the depth of suffering in the world. Typically, we don't have to look very far to see injustice, poverty, oppression, racism, and hatred.

And here's what's tricky: You may not think that those issues are prevalent in the area where you live. You might just look around every day and see kindness, fairness, and compassion in abundance. If that's the case, know that it is very rare indeed, and then consider the possibility of looking behind the scenes a little bit. Peek behind the curtain that separates your comfort from someone else's hardship. Hurting hearts are all around you, even if people can easily hide behind seemingly "normal" circumstances.

And know this: even if we legitimately feel like we live in a bubble, that doesn't exempt any of us from the responsibility of ministering to people in our communities, our nation, and our world. Needs are great, and resources are scarce. We certainly don't have to fix everything—we couldn't if we tried—but as people who profess faith in Jesus Christ, we should be ever-mindful and ever-prayerful of Micah 6:8:

> Mankind, he has told each of you what is good and what it is the LORD requires of you: to act justly, to love faithfulness, and to walk humbly with your God.

You might even say that we're called to be ambassadors of Micah 6:8. We should represent it no matter where we are. That doesn't mean that we try to help a bunch of people and promptly cast ourselves in the role of hero. Gospel-centered, gospel-driven ministry isn't the work of Captain America, after all. However, it does mean that we try to be more servant-like. That's the "walk humbly" part. And as we find joy in our service, as we prioritize someone else's needs above our own, we will more than likely find that we "love faithfulness" and kindness.

But how do you "act justly" in the middle of all the challenges in our current culture, especially if you're at a point in your life when you might not be on your own yet? Well, you have countless opportunities at your school or your job or within your own family to stand up for what's right and to serve as an advocate when someone's voice isn't being heard. After all, when we know the people we encounter in our daily routines are made in the image of God and should be treated as such, it changes how we respond. We're more likely to speak up and less likely to be idle bystanders. The Lord has given you a sound mind, a compassionate heart, and a strong voice; acting justly requires all three.

Today might be the perfect day to ask the Lord to show you how you can meet someone's needs in Jesus' name. What a gift to be a bridge-builder for the kingdom of God! And no matter what you're led to do, bow low and pray that, through your service, someone sees Jesus.

Or, better yet, that someone knows that Jesus sees her.

READ MATTHEW 5:1–11.

1. Do you tend to stay pretty aware of the injustices that surround you? Or do you sometimes fall into the trap of bubble-wrapping yourself or steering clear of difficult circumstances?

_____

_____

_____

2. When you think about how you can "act justly" in your own community, what comes to mind?

_____

_____

_____

3. When you think about how you can demonstrate mercy and kindness in your own community, what comes to mind?

_____

_____

_____

4. What are some specific ways you could minister to and be a voice for people who aren't necessarily heard?

_____

_____

_____

Today's Prayer

_____

_____

_____

_____

_____

_____

_____

_____

_____

_____

_____

_____

_____

Day 76

I grew up in a pretty average-sized church. There was no such thing as a mega-church at the time, of course, but there were definitely larger congregations in my hometown. At our church there were typically around a hundred seventy-five people in the sanctuary on Sunday mornings— maybe even three hundred at Christmas and Easter—and it seemed like a perfect size to me.

Now, of course, I'm a little (a lot) older, and our family belongs to a very big church. We average somewhere around twelve hundred people just in the eleven o'clock service, and between our three Sunday services, probably three thousand people worship at our church every week. A regular Sunday is ten times the size of an Easter Sunday crowd when I was growing up.

There's actually a good reason why I've been thinking about this particular topic. Last weekend I visited my hometown church for a special service, and there were maybe a hundred twenty-five folks sitting in the pews that were home to me for so many years.

Well, about ten minutes into the service, someone started to cough. The coughing was sporadic but persistent, and after the fourth or fifth coughing spell, I couldn't help but smile.

I know that probably sounds so strange, but my reaction was totally sincere. I meant it. Because this is the reality: when you're part of a smaller congregation and someone starts to cough, it's usually pretty easy to identify who might be having a hard time. It's easy to pass that person a mint or a cough drop. It's easy to check on him or her later.

And as I thought about the gentleman who was coughing a few pews over—about the care and concern he would no doubt encounter before he left that sanctuary—I thought, *Well, this is beautiful.*

It's not that we can't look out for each other in big churches. Of course we can. We do. But my Sunday morning in my hometown church reminded me of the grace of being able to take care of each other in small, everyday ways—like when someone is in the middle of a coughing fit, of all things—because, well, it means we're close enough to notice. It means we're close enough to help.

I'm certainly not trying to make a case for one kind of church being better than another. I'm just saying we don't have to lose the gift of small even if our church isn't. And in a world where we're often drawn to what's big and spacious and roomy—where we sometimes seek out environments where we have plenty of personal space—I think it's good for us to remember there are some real benefits when real life happens in quarters that are a little more cramped.

That doesn't mean you have to go to a smaller church. Maybe it just means you need to find a smaller group within your church where your coughing, so to speak, won't go unnoticed. Sure, it's not always comfortable. Sometimes you may long for a little more room to stretch and breathe. But as you check up on each other and take care of each other and share a cough drop or two, you'll see how something small—fueled by the hope of the gospel—can create something much bigger: big purpose, big mission, big love.

In Jesus' name.

READ ACTS 2:42-47.

1. What has your church experience been like in the past? Small church? Big church? No church? Talk about that a little bit.

2. Why do you think we can get so "antsy," for lack of a better word, about being in close community? Why does it bug us sometimes?

3. At this point in your life, are you part of a local church? Why or why not?

_____

_____

_____

4. How can our care for each other within the church affect and impact people outside the church?

_____

_____

_____

Today's Prayer

_____

_____

_____

_____

_____

_____

_____

_____

_____

_____

_____

_____

Day 11

*I*f you've ever sat under the leadership of someone you really admire, you know what a gift it is. Whether that person is a parent, a teacher, a coach, a small-group leader, or a boss, an excellent leader is someone who inspires, encourages, corrects, challenges, teaches, and motivates. That kind of leadership is a game-changer. In fact, when I look back over the course of my life, I can identify some major turning points that were directly related to the influence of kind, wise leaders. I imagine you could say the same.

From time to time, though, good leaders make bad decisions, and those bad decisions may result in a fall from leadership. If you've ever experienced the heartache that occurs when someone you deeply admire faces some sort of public failure, you know how surreal it can be. It might be that the leader was caught in secret sin, or he or she made an impulsive decision that resulted in a moral misstep. Maybe the public persona and the private person didn't match up, and the façade couldn't bear the weight of leadership. Whatever the reason—and there are thousands of ways to fall—there's no doubt that it's surreal to see someone we admire wage a private battle in the midst of public disgrace.

Ultimately, however—regardless of the whos and hows and whys—there are some very practical responses to a leader's troubles that will serve us well while honoring the person who is struggling:

1. **Humility.** We sometimes put leaders on pedestals and forget that they're human, like us. Not one of us is less susceptible to failure or somehow immune to it. So, if we think for one second that there is any sin beyond our grasp, we're kidding ourselves. From that perspective a leader's public failure should remind us to put away our pointed finger and instead look inward, asking the Lord to "see if there is any offensive way in me; lead me in the everlasting way" (Psalm 139:24).

2. **Prayer.** We live smack dab in the middle of a 24-hour news cycle, not to mention that the Internet gives us around-the-clock access

to the court of public opinion via social media comments. We're exposed to an enormous amount of information that may or may not be true. That's precisely why our wisest course of action is to resist the urge to play investigative reporter and pray instead. Pray for healing, for hope, for peace, and for restoration. Remember, God is good at redeeming.

3. **Gratitude.** Cynicism has a way of creeping in when we find out that someone we admire is struggling behind-the-scenes. But instead of being disillusioned, be grateful. Remember all that person taught you, and be thankful for the difference he or she made in your life. Even if current circumstances seem unpleasant or discouraging, they can't change the fact that the Lord allowed that leader to make a difference in your life. That's cause for gratitude.

In the Lord's providence, some leaders are only in our lives for a season. It's unfortunate when that season ends before we think we're ready, or if it ends in a way that leaves us feeling confused or hurt. God's faithfulness, however, cannot be undone or diminished by people's mistakes. Hang in there. Pray like crazy. And remember that even though leaders may let us down, our Father in heaven never will.

READ MICAH 7:18–20.

1. Who are some leaders you really admire?

2. What are some qualities you see in those people that stand out to you?

3. Do you have a tendency to put leaders on a pedestal? Or do you feel a certain amount of skepticism about people in leadership? Think about that for a minute, and write down your thoughts.

4. Can you think of any leaders in the Bible who let people down? Did their ministries still make a difference?

Today's Prayer

Day 78

The school where I work has a chapel service once a week, and one of the cool things about that time with the faculty and the student body is that our worship team is made up of students. It's so encouraging to walk into the auditorium and know I'm going to be led by some of the kids I get to hang out with and work with every day. And singing two or three songs together is typically one of the best parts of my Thursdays.

Last week we started chapel by singing a song called "Forever Reign." If you're active in a youth group, you've probably sung the same song once or forty-eight times. The words are super familiar to me at this point, so I sang my way through the first few verses and the chorus, and to be honest, it probably wasn't my finest moment of worshiping "in Spirit and in truth" (John 4:24). I was distracted by some folks who were switching seats a couple of rows ahead of me, I was slightly worried about the previous day's election news, and I was simultaneously running through a mental to-do list of what I needed to accomplish that afternoon.

Basically I was a textbook example of what *not* to do in worship. It's the weirdest thing: although you might think that as you get older you won't have to fight to focus all your attention and affection on the Lord during worship, guess what, everybody? I was basically about four seconds away from pulling my phone out of my pocket and checking Twitter.

But here's why we need to stay in it with worship when we're discouraged: because about one second before I surrendered to Chapel Twitter Time (NOT RECOMMENDED, by the way), the lyrics from the bridge section of "Forever Reign"—lyrics that proclaimed that the name of Jesus was the only name I would sing—started to pierce my heart.

In that moment two things happened at the same time: I was deeply moved by the strong declaration coming from every part of the auditorium as students sang those same words, *and* I was deeply convicted about all the other names my heart had sung throughout the week.

I mean, I could stand there and sing that there's no other name than Jesus all I wanted to, but the fact of the matter was that my heart had sung lots of names over the previous seventy-two-ish hours:

Me, me
Fear, fear
Doubt, doubt
Frustration, frustration
Pride, pride

We could pretty much sit here for the rest of the day and break down all the idols that had infiltrated my week. But I think you get the point.

And here's the great big grace of worship: as I stood there under the conviction of the Holy Spirit, I bowed my head, silently confessed my sin to the Lord, and asked Him to forgive me. And you'd better believe that as we continued to sing that section of the song several more times, I was fully engaged: heart, soul, and mind. It wasn't that I needed to have all my problems solved before I walked into chapel. I just needed to get honest.

It's okay to struggle, y'all. It's okay to sit or stand or kneel before the Lord and know that you need His help to set things right. Praise Him for the never-ending, astonishing grace of second, third, and 859th chances. He's so good to us.

READ 1 JOHN 1:5–10.

1. What are some of the idols that have infiltrated your heart this past week? What are some of the names your heart has sung?

2. Has there been a recent time in worship when you've felt convicted (or encouraged) by the words you were singing? Explain.

3. Is confession a regular part of your time with the Lord?

4. Is there any area of your life where you feel like you're "playing Christian"? Any area where it might do your heart good to get honest before the Lord?

Today's Prayer

Day 79

*E*very once in a while, you'll come across a subject in school where everything just clicks. You understand the material pretty easily, you enjoy what you're learning, and you relish the feeling of continually improving in that particular area. For whatever reason, the content makes sense to you in the most natural, enjoyable way.

I can tell you without hesitation that Algebra II was not that subject for me.

Even though I'd done well in Algebra I, I was immediately aware that Algebra II was not going to be my happy place. I took notes and nodded my head like I was following along with every factor and formula just fine, but I might as well have been conjugating verbs in hieroglyphics. (Do you even conjugate hieroglyphics verbs? I have no idea. But the point is that Algebra II was like an ancient language I'd never before encountered.)

Now there were all sorts of ways I could have managed my math struggle more proactively and effectively. I could have asked my teacher for help. I could have gotten a tutor. I could have thrown myself at the mercy of my classmates and begged them to help me.

Here's what I did: nothing. I had so many questions, but I was too afraid to ask. The fact that everybody else seemed to understand effortlessly made me feel dumb, honestly. I was totally lost, and as far as algebra was concerned, insecurity and fear hovered over me like a leaning tower of polynomials.

Every single day, however, I sat in my desk and nodded my head and acted like I knew what was going on. I was a professional pretender when I was in class. My grades told the real story, though.

And I tell you all that because I think lots of us operate the same way when it comes to our faith. In fact, when I was younger, I *absolutely* operated that way in terms of my faith. Even after I became a believer (maybe even *especially* after I became a believer), I had so many questions, so much doubt, and I wasn't sure how the Bible answered (or didn't answer) the stuff I didn't know. But instead of talking to my parents or asking my youth group leader or seeking out a mentor, I went to church every single Sunday and sat in our regular pew and nodded my head and acted like I understood.

I was a professional pretender when it came to growing in my faith. My life told the real story, though.

And the common denominator in both of these situations?

Pride.

Pride is almost always the primary deterrent to vulnerability. Pride lies to us and convinces us that shame is just around the corner if we confess how we're struggling. But we don't have to be afraid to ask hard questions. We don't have to be intimidated by what we don't know. We certainly don't have to feel ashamed for not having all the answers. So as you grow and mature in your walk with the Lord, speak up. Ask away. Listen carefully.

The Lord will meet you and teach you no matter where you are in your walk with Him. And you won't even have to factor a thing.

READ MATTHEW 7:7–11.

1. Do you find it pretty easy to ask others for help? Or are you more likely to nod and play along and pretend like everything is under control?

_____

_____

_____

2. Have you ever wrestled with some hard questions or some doubt in terms of your faith? Explain.

_____

_____

_____

3. Is there any part of your life where you're currently puzzled but pretending? (And if it's something like Algebra II, go right ahead and talk about that. It doesn't have to be something spiritual.)

4. Seeking after Truth is always worth it. Look at Psalm 143:6, and write it down here.

Today's Prayer

Day 80

When I was growing up there was a big cultural push to build up kids' self-esteem. The rationale was that if young people felt better about themselves, they'd behave better, perform better, interact with others better. And for the last twenty-five or so years, that whole notion of cultivating self-esteem has been the foundation for countless parenting and self-help books.

These days we still hear about self-esteem (which, in my opinion, greatly pales in comparison to the importance of understanding our identity in Christ) and the perils of the lack of it, but there's a much bigger issue in play. I didn't even have words for this particular problem until a few days ago when my friend Amy mentioned it. But I'm convinced that, if left unchecked, it's going to damage relationships, hurt families, and continue to hold countless young women in its grip.

That sounds pretty dramatic, doesn't it? Well, it should. Because it's dangerous. And what is it, you wonder?

Self-worship. It is absolutely, one hundred percent a real thing.

Just think about the vast amounts of time young women can spend looking at themselves in the mirror, taking selfies, adding filters, and editing pictures. Then there are the seemingly endless ways people try to tweak and manage their own stinkin' image, and while some of that is because of too much focus on perceived faults, mostly it's for the glory of *me, myself, and I.*

And although we could sit here and point fingers at this celebrity and that reality star and some other social media phenomenon as the causes, we'd be better off taking time to carefully examine how self-worship is affecting our *own* lives. Consider how tempting it is to see our lives as something to be curated as opposed to just lived, and it's easy to see how we've gotten off-track. Everybody is potentially the star in his or her own reality show—broadcast courtesy of Instagram or Snapchat or the platform of your choice—and being a star is a lot of work. There's a reputation to build and protect, after all, so how a person presents her life becomes strategic. She needs to look a certain way, dress a certain way, smile a certain way, and she also needs to be seen with the right people. Her followers would expect no less, right?

To be clear, I get it. And I realize that most of us aren't deliberately crafting a social media presence. Even still, the bent toward self-worship lurks behind the scenes in our heads and our hearts. That's why we have to be brutally honest with ourselves and brutally honest before the Lord as we answer some key questions.

- Am I living to glorify myself?
- Am I more concerned with myself than anything else?
- Am I spending my days trying to build and further my own reputation?
- Do I filter my life to make it look like something it isn't?
- Do I present my life as a brand or my body as a product?
- Do I live like the queen of my own tiny kingdom?

And listen. I don't want to be an alarmist. It can be fun to have a following. It can be a neat experience when younger girls look up to you, or when other girls think you'd be a trustworthy friend. But if you're intentionally creating that, buying into that, or believing your own press, so to speak, you'd be wise to shut it down sooner as opposed to later.

Bottom line: if nothing is more important to you than you, consider the possibility that you've elevated yourself to a place where you were never meant to be. You are a beautiful, blood-bought child of the Most High God, and I say this in all love: the Lord is the only One who is worthy of our worship and adoration. We're not built for it, we can't handle it, and we're foolish to think that we have any claim to sit on His throne.

READ EXODUS 20:3-6.

1. What are some specific ways you see the prevalence of self-worship in our culture?

2. Do you edit or enhance pictures of yourself before you post them online?

_____

_____

3. Have you ever fallen into the trap of prioritizing yourself above your relationship with the Lord? How'd that work out?

_____

_____

4. Look at the six questions you read earlier. Are you concerned about or convicted by any of your answers?

_____

_____

Today's Prayer

_____

_____

_____

_____

_____

_____

_____

_____

_____

_____

Day 81

Since I have a job where I'm sort of an on-campus mama to junior high and high school girls, people naturally assume that I deal with lots of crying on a weekly basis. Sometimes I guess that's true—maybe during a week when there are lots of tests or students are feeling particularly stressed—but for the most part, I've noticed, teenage girls don't cry about their own problems as often as people might think.

That's not to say that teenage girls don't cry. Of course they do. But what I've noticed—and what has surprised me a little bit—is that so many times when I'm talking with a girl who is emotional or crying, it's because she's feeling those things for someone else. She's upset because a friend is having a hard time, or a parent is fighting a health-related battle, or she wishes she could take on a struggle that a younger sibling is facing.

In other words, the grief and the sorrow aren't necessarily self-focused. Many times they're other-focused. And although that doesn't necessarily make it easy or pleasant for the person who is experiencing the sadness, there are a few reasons why I remind girls to be encouraged that the Lord is at work in the middle of the heartache and the tears, regardless of the cause:

1. **Your heart is tender.** It might sound trite or obvious, but never underestimate the gift of a tender heart. It is far too easy in this world to become callous or hard-hearted, so shedding tears and feeling brokenhearted lets you know you have not closed yourself off to the suffering and hardship that surrounds you. A tender heart enables you to be responsive and minister to others.
2. **The Lord is building empathy in you.** It's a great thing to be able to feel. It's even better to be able to put yourself in someone else's shoes and see the world from his or her perspective. When you hurt for your friends, you're doing just that. You're empathizing. You're sharing in their burdens and demonstrating great compassion. That is a gift from the Lord. Anyone who wants to

lead well, serve well, or love well will greatly benefit from the ability to empathize.

3. **You're learning how to take care of your people.** One of the hardest parts of friendship—or any relationship, really—is figuring out how to meet individual needs, especially when someone you love is in the middle of a difficult time. There's a delicate balance between empathy and action, and as you cry and question and whatever else is helpful as you grieve, the Lord is teaching you how to move through your own emotions while keeping someone else's needs at the forefront. This is a high-level skill when it comes to emotional maturity. What a blessing to be able to cultivate that skill while you're young.

It never gets easier to see friends and family members in physical or emotional pain, and it can be overwhelming to care for them as we hurt with them. However, the Lord is gracious to put us in situations where we can learn, grow, and mature. We'll rarely be able to fix someone else's problems, but we can most certainly be loving, compassionate friends.

READ 2 CORINTHIANS 1:3–7.

1. Have you ever cried over someone else's suffering? Explain.

_____

_____

2. Where would you say you rank on an empathy scale? Low, medium, or high? How do you know?

_____

_____

_____

3. What are some ways the Lord has comforted you when you've gone through a hard time?

4. Look up Galatians 6:2. Write, illustrate, or doodle it here.

Today's Prayer

Day 82

*O*ver the last few months my mama's Bible has become one of my most treasured possessions. I brought it back to Birmingham after she passed away, and every morning, after I make a cup of coffee and sit down at our kitchen table, I open her Bible and immediately feel connected to her memory and her legacy. The pages even smell like her hand lotion—she flipped through those pages for more than twenty years, after all—and since Mama liked to underline as she read, her Bible is like a journal of what the Lord was teaching her. No matter what verse I look up, my eye goes straight to whatever Mama underlined in red or black ink (sometimes both—if she revisited a certain passage).

I don't have any reason to believe that she planned it, but Mama's faithful Scripture reading and underlining has brought me such comfort after her death. It's made my confidence that she's with her heavenly Father even sweeter. And there's been an additional blessing I never expected: certain themes have emerged as I've read the verses Mama underlined. It's fascinating, really. Over and over Mama underlined passages about the assurance of salvation, the power of the tongue, and the necessity of humility.

And here's what occurred to me a few days ago: Mama is still teaching me.

Now there's no doubt that our parents spend their whole lives teaching us. It starts early, too, when they plead with us not to run around the pool or stick our finger in the light socket or put glue in our hair. Then we learn to play fair at sports and obey our authorities and honor our elders. As we get older we hear admonitions to look after our friends and drive carefully and work our hardest at everything we do. Then we leave home and get out on our own and the lessons keep coming: always put God first, spend and save wisely, and invest your time in your community. It doesn't matter how old we are or how old our parents are, that dynamic is almost always there.

I just never expected how rich it would continue to be—even after Mama went to heaven.

But in the Lord's kindness, I reacquaint myself with Mama's legacy every single morning when I open her Bible. I see the notes she took, the passages she loved, and the lists she made. I see that her relationship with the Lord was more intimate than I ever imagined, and her trust in the righteousness of Jesus was rock solid. I see that she faithfully prayed for her family and friends. I see that she truly enjoyed life with Jesus while she was here on earth, but her deepest desire—expressed over and over again on the pages of her Bible—was to enjoy eternity with Him in heaven.

When I consider how I've been schooled by grief over the last few months, it's no wonder every single one of these lessons has been beyond precious to me. I had no idea how much I needed to learn them. I had no idea how the Lord would use that knowing to give me peace.

No matter how much you may think you wish otherwise, you are never, ever too old for the wisdom of people who faithfully speak into your life. You can't even imagine how you'll treasure it down the road and how you'll continue to seek it when they're no longer in your life on a daily basis. In so many ways I never anticipated, my mama's wisdom is a priceless gift that, thankfully, keeps on giving.

READ PSALM 78:1-4.

1. Do you have any treasures that belonged to older relatives or loved ones? Maybe a Bible, old letters, or journals?

2. Have you ever been surprised by anything you've learned about older relatives or loved ones? Explain.

3. At this point in your life, whose legacy means the most to you? Who is the older person in your life who seems to have passed on the most wisdom or encouragement to you?

_____

_____

_____

4. What will you want to tell your children about your parents? Your grandparents?

_____

_____

_____

Today's Prayer

_____

_____

_____

_____

_____

_____

_____

_____

_____

_____

_____

_____

Day 83

*N*ot too long ago my husband and I, along with our small group, watched a video about marriage. The speaker started his talk by mentioning some of the little things that can make marriage frustrating, and as he transitioned into the bigger message, he offered the audience what I think he intended to be comforting and reassuring:

"God wants you to be happy," he said.

Every single one of us turned our eyes from the TV screen to each other. To be honest, every single one of us looked a little confused. We eventually turned our attention back to the video, but after it was over and we settled into our discussion time, the question came up: "So. Does God *really* want us to be happy?"

Because here's a news flash: there's not a single instance in Scripture where God mentions that He has prioritized our happiness *or* that our happiness is the primary point of a life surrendered to Christ.

In fact, that's a place where we can get really tangled up when it comes to living a life of faith. We tell ourselves that God wants us to be happy, and our quest for happiness can lead us to make some short-term, rash, selfish decisions that ripple in ways we never intended.

And sorry, by the way, if that sounds a little doom and gloom. But I guess what I'm trying to say is that happiness is mostly a by-product of stuff that's temporary, and God never indicates that it should be our highest aim. Happiness is when you get a 40-percent-off coupon for your favorite cosmetics brand. Happiness is when you've had a long day at school and you get home and your mama has cooked your favorite meal. Happiness is when you're with two of your closest friends and you laugh so hard you can't speak. All of those things are wonderful and enjoyable, for sure.

But God has so much more for us than mere happiness. Here's a list just for starters.

- He enables us to be joyful at all times. (Philippians 4:4)
- He gives us peace that passes all understanding. (Philippians 4:7)
- He teaches us to be content in any circumstances. (Philippians 4:12)
- He compels us to be faithful with our whole lives. (Revelation 2:10)
- He calls us to be holy because He is holy. (1 Peter 1:15)

We live in a world with a subjective view of truth, and with that comes a mentality that our happiness is paramount. I hope you'll hear my heart when I tell you that that's a load of lies. A life focused primarily on personal happiness can result in a selfishly shallow existence that is far too dependent on circumstances.

However, a life focused on the joy of the Lord and the gifts of the Spirit can lead to a God-centered, meaningful existence that is rooted in unchanging Truth.

Don't settle for chasing happy. God has so much more in store for you.

READ GALATIANS 5:22-26.

1. To be clear, there's nothing wrong with happiness. Heavens, no. It's just more dependent on circumstances than joy is. So given that, what are some temporary things that *do* bring you happiness? (And yes, it is totally fine if some form of ice cream is one of your answers.)

2. Now that you've thought about what makes you happy, think about what brings you deep joy. What are some of those things? Explain if necessary.

3. Do you notice a contrast between the first list and the second list? How would you explain the difference?

_____

_____

_____

4. According to Romans 15:13, joy and peace lead to _____. Why is that so needed and necessary in our current culture?

_____

_____

_____

Today's Prayer

_____

_____

_____

_____

_____

_____

_____

_____

_____

_____

_____

_____

_____

Day 84

I'm a leadership junkie.

That doesn't mean I am addicted to leading. It just means I love watching people lead. I haven't always been that way—in fact, I don't think I gave leadership a second's thought for the first forty years of my life—but over the last few years, I've been fascinated by how people lead, why people follow, what qualities good leaders share, and pretty much all the leadership things.

So given my deep affection for strong leadership, it might surprise you to know one of the very best examples I have ever seen. It was a pop superstar performing at a Country Music Association Awards show. True story.

So first of all, let me set the stage. At the time, this superstar was coming off of a mega-successful world tour and was basically king of the world (okay, not really a king, but definitely in a can-do-no-wrong stage of his career). It was a huge deal for him to be performing at the CMAs, and he took the time to do so with a rising country star whose career was just getting off the ground (although he'd been a successful songwriter for many years). They seemed like an unlikely pair.

But oh, y'all. From the first note of their performance, it was obvious that something special was happening. I won't even attempt to give you the play-by-play, but by the time they finished singing, I was standing in front of the television (I moved closer and closer throughout the performance) and thinking, *Well, that was pretty much a master class in leadership.*

Here's why.

1. **The leader was in control.** There was no question that the pop superstar knew where that performance was heading, and he knew how to get there. There are several times when you can see the new country singer look his way for direction or for a cue, and he got it. A good leader is trustworthy and responsive.
2. **The leader continually checked in with his team.** Over and over during those seven minutes, the superstar turned to

his bandleader and musicians. Sometimes he'd walk in their direction, and sometimes he'd stay put, but there was constant communication and encouragement. A good leader builds collaboration.

3. **The leader wasn't afraid to share the spotlight.** There's one moment in particular where the superstar was primed for his biggest note of the night—he had the audience in the palm of his hand—and instead of hitting the note himself, he looked across the stage at his partner and said, "Take it!" It was like he passed the ball when he could have shot a three-pointer. And in that moment, the country singer shined. It was beautiful. A good leader feels no need to hog the spotlight.

Maybe my favorite moment was after the performance. The audience was going crazy, but if you looked closely at the stage, you could see that every single person was focused on someone else. The musicians, the back-up singers, the bandleader, and the performers were all cheering each other on, all commending one another. No one was trying to be the center of attention.

Most of us will never sing at an awards show, but we will, at some point, be called to lead in our schools, churches, and workplaces. So remember: servant leadership pushes every team member in the direction of God's best. It spurs people on in their callings. It values others and doesn't need credit. It's rooted in humility, and it bears beautiful fruit.

Thanks, Talented Music People, for the lesson.

READ MARK 10:42-45.

1. Can you think of a public figure—a singer, athlete, actor, whoever— who strikes you as an excellent leader?

2. When you think of "quiet confidence," does anyone come to mind?

_____

_____

3. Are you more likely to respond to a leader with quiet confidence or one who's more outwardly and loudly confident?

_____

_____

4. Have you ever thought about your own leadership style? Are you more of a boss or a coach? Or would you rather delegate?

_____

_____

Today's Prayer

_____

_____

_____

_____

_____

_____

_____

_____

_____

_____

_____

_____

Day 85

I was nineteen, probably, when it hit me for the first time. I was a sophomore in college, active on campus, doing well in school, surrounded by phenomenal friends—and every day I battled deep, gnawing sadness that I could not shake for the life of me. It didn't matter how much my friends encouraged me, or how many cute notes they left on my dorm room door, or how often I reminded myself that I was loved and safe and relationally fulfilled. I was sad, and the sad wouldn't leave.

Logically I knew that my family and my friends loved me, but I almost always felt like nobody really *saw* me. It sounds pretty needy when I look back on it, but wanting attention wasn't the issue. I had no desire to sit in the center of a circle while people affirmed me. (By the way, that scenario continues to hold strong on my top 10 list of PLEASE NEVER LET THIS HAPPEN.) The issue was that I felt left out of my own life, if that makes sense. I could objectively look at the friends and the activities and the fun and think, *Wow, this is awesome! I should be having the time of my life!* But in the weirdest way, I didn't feel like I was part of any of it.

Good times, right?

I never thought I was depressed; I didn't have any trouble sticking to my routine or finishing my work or anything like that. I didn't feel hopeless. I mostly felt super lonely, and eventually, the lonely lifted. But what I've learned since then is that when I'm in transition—whether that's moving or changing jobs or figuring out how to navigate a new stage of parenting or whatever—the "sad and lonely" tends to pay me a visit. Sometimes it's an extended one. And while I can't say that it's my favorite, I can say that the Lord has taught me a few lessons in the middle of it. Here are three:

1. **"Sad and lonely" leads me to examine my true identity in Christ.** Even when I feel like a stranger in my own life, Jesus is for me. He is with me. He is my intercessor and my advocate. My feelings don't define me, nor do my circumstances. Only Jesus. He sees me and loves me. He is continually working all things for good—even the sadness.

2. **"Sad and lonely" helps me appreciate the blessing of community.** There's something surreal about being in a bout with sadness and having people in your life who continue to show up and reach out and love you right there in the middle of it. It's strangely beautiful that, when nothing seems more appealing than good, old-fashioned isolation, the people in your life won't have it. They're a constant chorus of "Nope, sister, you're with us." And it helps. It really does.

3. **"Sad and lonely" reminds me that this world is not my home.** The older I get, the more I recognize that this world isn't built to satisfy, and if we're living lives that are surrendered to Jesus, we're going to feel out of place and out of sorts from time to time. That's okay. Our hearts really do long for "a better country, that is, a heavenly one" (Hebrews 11:16 ESV). As wonderful as this life is, it doesn't compare to our eternal home. In some way our sadness and loneliness remind us that we're longing for the country we haven't seen.

And here's some unsolicited advice: if you can't shake the "sad and lonely," or if you've gone a step beyond it and suspect that you're depressed, today is a great day to tell someone who loves you. We're never as alone as we fear. Thank You, Jesus.

READ ROMANS 8:31–39.

1. Do you ever struggle with sadness or loneliness?

_____

_____

2. Are there any common denominators in the times you battle the "sad and lonely"? Any specific situations that seem to cause it?

_____

3. Are you more likely to feel sad when you're at home? At school? When you're scrolling through social media? Some other time?

4. According to Philippians 3:20, where is our citizenship?

Today's Prayer

Day 86

*I*t occurs to me that it's typically pretty easy to be a good Christian when you're at some form of church retreat. You play some holy dodge ball (or Ping-Pong or Four Square), you go for a hike, you sing the worship songs, you dig into Scripture, you pray for and with your friends, and by the time you leave, you're all *Yay, God! I am so on fire for Jesus, y'all! Would someone like to go riding around so we can sing "Oceans" at the top of our lungs?*

But then you go home, and real life hits. You find out that your little sister "borrowed" your favorite sweater for the twenty-fourth time. Your parents want to talk about that C you have in biology. You remember that you have an essay due, and you haven't even figured out the topic you're going to write about yet. You're annoyed.

And then you're at lunch the next day, and there's a conversation about a political candidate or a controversial issue, and you just lose it. You are so frustrated, in fact, that the word *enraged* comes to mind. And when you consider everything that's happened in the seventeen or eighteen hours since you left the retreat, you think, *Well, Jesus does not appear to be on the premises. He has in fact left the building. And it is probably because He overheard me arguing about some political crisis, and He took issue with my tone.*

That tension between spiritual highs and real life can be something else, can't it? And to be perfectly clear: it's always going to be a thing. It just is. It's the intersection of the vertical life (the stuff that goes on between us and God) and the horizontal life (the stuff that goes on as we attempt to live out our faith in the world). If we could live a perfect cross-centered, cross-driven life in our own strength, we would have no need for Jesus. Jesus was and is and will be the only way—*the only Way*—to bridge the gap between the horizontal and the vertical. We can't do it on our own.

So if I could, let me encourage you a little bit today:

1. **It's good that you're aware of the tension.** In fact, it's huge. That awareness is your assurance that the Holy Spirit is convicting you and prompting you in the most mundane parts of real life. It's

assurance that you don't need a cathedral to hear from Him. It's assurance that you're not okay to just let your faith go sideways in the real world. Jesus is at work in you.

2. **You're never going to get it exactly right.** We're all desperately imperfect, and we're all sinners. And if you're thinking, *Well, that's not very encouraging*, I promise it actually is. Because when we get a glimmer of real life that feels as much like worship to us as our time singing in a sanctuary, we know that can only be the power of Jesus at work in us. He does what we can't. He does what we wouldn't apart from His ongoing grace in our lives. He's bridging the gap for us.

3. **Jesus never stops teaching us.** Think of the most patient teacher you've ever had. Then multiply that level of patience by a thousand. Then square it. And quadruple it. You still aren't anywhere close to the level of patience Jesus has with us. He's going to continue to convict you, refine you, and call you higher. He knows that resolving the tension between the vertical and horizontal is lifelong work for us, but He's committed to the process. He's committed to you.

Thank Him for His patience today.

READ 1 PETER 2:9–12.

1. When you think of times you've been on the spiritual mountaintop, so to speak, what comes to mind?

2. Have you ever been aware of how your real-life faith can look very different than those mountaintop moments? Explain.

3. Do you ever battle feelings of hypocrisy when it comes to your faith? Why? How do you handle that?

_____

_____

_____

4. Look up John 1:16. Write, doodle, or illustrate it here.

_____

_____

_____

_____

Today's Prayer

_____

_____

_____

_____

_____

_____

_____

_____

_____

_____

_____

_____

Day 87

This is merely a theory, but I'm halfway convinced that at some point there was an anonymous committee that got together and decided that high school seniors couldn't possibly graduate unless they were prepared to lay out a detailed ten-year plan complete with college options, internship goals, post-graduate degree strategies, and contact information for their top ten preferred employers. I'm not sure when it started, but across the board we're placing an enormous amount of responsibility on high school and college-aged students to, like, FIGURE IT OUT ALREADY.

As someone who picked a college major based on *how I liked to spend my spare time* (writing) and then pretty much skipped off to college with no real plan, I'm a little awed by the present-day trend of mapping out the future when you're eighteen years old. It's a whole lot of pressure, right? More and more it feels like we're expecting high school seniors to somehow have the foresight of a seasoned CEO and create what essentially amounts to a business plan for their lives.

So listen closely to what I'm about to tell you: *You don't have to do that.*

You don't. You don't have to know what's four or six or twelve years down the road. You don't have to forecast how the marketplace will accommodate your potential major over the next fifteen years. You don't have to figure out where you're going to grad school before you've completed your first college course.

All you have to know is this: *What is the wise, right, God-honoring next step in your life?*

Granted, that's a pretty big question all by itself. But it's a question you can answer under the counsel and covering of your parents and/or trusted leaders in your life. And when you really pray through that one question—when you really start to look through a lens of wisdom and honoring the Lord—you may start to see lots more options:

- Maybe it's wise for you to take a gap year to serve others and mature in your faith.

- Maybe it's wise to work part-time to offset tuition costs.
- Maybe it's wise to take a few core classes at a community college to see what interests you before you commit to a major.

There really are countless *maybe*s, but you'll never consider them if you commit to the plan you've created without prayerfully seeking the Lord's plan for the next right thing.

And listen. I get it. You don't want to miss opportunities because you neglected to plan ahead. There's definitely a balance with that, and that's why you need to seek out sound advice. But by the same token, you don't want to be so locked in to a plan you've made that you fail to heed the prompting of the Holy Spirit. You don't want to miss the Lord's leading.

So take a deep breath. Sit down with a couple of people you really trust. Seek direction from Scripture and prayer. Commit to God's best for your life—no matter what that looks like. Following Him is the adventure of a lifetime, and it's infinitely better than anything you could map out on your own.

READ HEBREWS 13:17–21.

1. Do you feel any pressure in regard to your future? Why do you think that is (or isn't)?

_____

_____

2. Have you ever dismissed a possibility for your future—like studying abroad or taking a gap year—because it seemed too unconventional or even impossible?

_____

_____

_____

3. Do you feel bound by other people's expectations for your future? Or do you feel total freedom? Explain.

4. Can you honestly say that you trust the Lord with the details of your future? Or do you like to "help" Him a little bit? (I was smiling as I typed that. Promise.)

Today's Prayer

Day 88

I think we can probably agree that everybody has a bad day from time to time. Whether we wake up grumpy or get stuck in traffic or realize that we're not at all prepared for whatever the day holds, we all have those instances when we're a little more annoyed than usual, and naturally those less-than-stellar moods can carry over into our friendships.

Given all of that, we shouldn't be surprised if there's a day or two out of the year when one of our friends isn't as talkative, seems slightly more sensitive, or reacts a little more strongly than might be typical for her. It happens. And since we've all been there, it's easy to understand why we can and should extend some grace in those kinds of situations.

But what if the bad moods and the higher levels of drama become increasingly normal for a friend? What if you find yourself on the receiving end of a friend's temper over and over again? What if someone has morphed into a mean girl you hardly recognize anymore? How do you respond when someone is frequently unkind—maybe even manipulative—either on social media or in real life, and you have no idea what you did to make her so angry?

Let's talk about that for a second.

And let's talk about it with the assumption that you haven't intentionally or unintentionally done anything to hurt this person (because if you have, then a good first step is always to apologize and make sure there's no unspoken tension between the two of you).

All righty. So. Here's the main thing to remember if you're running into "mean girl" problems at school or at work or wherever:

As a general rule, people don't lash out, act out, or stir up drama when they stand confidently in their identity in Christ.

Please know that I say that in the most tender, loving way. Because any time you unwillingly get dragged onto the mean girl roller coaster, you have to remind yourself that it isn't about a person being "bad" or "mean." It isn't because you've done anything wrong. It's usually because the person who starts the drama is fearful, insecure, and consciously or unconsciously dealing with those feelings by trying to make someone else feel worse.

And then there's this: sometimes people mistake meanness for power. And power, for whatever reason, becomes the way they measure their social status and standing.

So if you find yourself trying to keep the peace with someone who seems perfectly content to stay mired in the muck of meanness, know that her behavior has nothing to do with you. You haven't asked for it, you don't deserve it, and you shouldn't waste energy or emotion trying to fix it. You can be kind, of course—ask the Lord to help you preserve the integrity of your testimony, to be a listening ear in the event of sincere repentance— but you get to have boundaries too. You have no reason to be afraid or walk on eggshells. You have no reason to retaliate.

Guard your heart. Stay grounded in the Word. Spend time with the Lord. Focus your energy on friendships that are healthy and drama-free. Never lose sight of how the Lord might redeem and restore what's broken. Never forget who you are in Him.

READ PSALM 34:1-10.

1. Have you ever had to deal with mean girls? What was that experience like?

2. Have you ever been aware that you were behaving like a mean girl? How did you respond to that realization?

3. Don't get offended, and really think through this: Even if you wouldn't have considered yourself a mean girl, do you think you've ever been perceived as one? Why or why not?

4. Do you think social media helps or hurts with "mean girl" behavior? Explain.

Today's Prayer

Day 89

$\mathcal{B}$ack in the late 00's, a worship song called "How He Loves" took the church by storm.

Okay. That sounded a little weird. Because it wasn't like, you know, if Bruno Mars showed up at a mall or anything like that. But it was one of those songs where it seemed like everybody was talking about it all at once. It was a big deal, and I am really over explaining considering that I haven't gotten anywhere near my main point yet.

Anyhoo.

So the other day I was reading Psalm 139, and after verse 12, I stopped for a second and looked back over what I'd read. There's reference after reference to the fact that David can't make a move without the Lord being aware of it. In just the first three verses, in fact, we see "you have searched me and known me," "you understand my thoughts," "you are aware of all my ways." And I think that if Psalm 139 were a super-popular worship song, a really good title would be "How He Knows."

(See what I did there?)

But then I had another thought: *We don't always want to be known like that.*

If we're totally honest, that level of knowing can make us a little itchy. And there are plenty of reasons why.

For one thing, we fear rejection from God. We expect that anyone who knows our innermost thoughts, anyone who can see the deepest parts of our heart—well, they will surely reject us, right? I mean, no one could see all that sin and ugliness and pettiness and spite and still want to be in relationship with us.

Another reason we don't want to be known like that is that we enjoy feeling self-sufficient. We like the illusion that we're in control and don't necessarily have to answer to anyone (much less the Sovereign King of the universe) for our thoughts and our actions. Sometimes we much prefer the idea that we're all in charge of our own tiny kingdoms.

And one more reason? The Lord's love doesn't always make sense to us. Our human capacity for love is fickle. We're swayed by circumstances, we're motivated by pride, and we're prone to selfishness. We try to put God's love in a human context and cast Him in the role of Holy Scorekeeper—but that's not His deal at all. God loves lavishly. Completely. Selflessly. Endlessly. His love isn't on a sliding scale based on our behavior either. Even in our darkest moments, He continues to cover us in unfailing love. If we could comprehend the depth of His love for just the tiniest amount of time, we would delight in how He knows us. We would find such comfort in His unconditional care.

You are fully, completely, and joyfully known by the God of the Universe. He delights in you. He treasures you. He knows you completely—and He absolutely adores you.

Thank Him for that today.

READ PSALM 139:1–12.

1. Who knows you better than anyone else? It might be a relative, or it might be a friend, but just jot his or her name below.

_____

_____

2. Do you have any secrets in that relationship? I'm not talking about anything dark and scandalous, necessarily, just pieces of yourself that you keep hidden?

_____

_____

_____

3. How does it make you feel when you think about the fact that the Lord knows every single thing about you? Every thought? Every action? Every intention? Is that a comfort to you? Or does it make you feel vulnerable to know that nothing is hidden?

_____

_____

4. Just in case you struggle with remembering how much the Lord loves you, read Psalm 86:15 and then write it down here.

_____

_____

Today's Prayer

_____

_____

_____

_____

_____

_____

_____

_____

_____

_____

_____

Day 90

*I*t's easy to content ourselves with belief.

Here's what I mean. We can, without even realizing it, develop a personal faith checklist, and when all the boxes are checked, we decide we're covered on the faith stuff. It might look something like this:

- believe God is real
- read Bible
- join a church
- try to be a good person

And let me be so clear: those are all good things. It's just that none of those things on their own has the power to save us from our sin.

Here's why:

There's a big difference between a life that acknowledges God and a life that's surrendered to Him.

Think about it in the context of everyday life. When you acknowledge someone, you basically assent to his or her existence. Your acknowledgment essentially means *Yes, you are here, and I see you.*

Surrender, however, is a whole different deal. Acknowledgment is certainly the first part of it, but there's a much deeper piece—and peace (see what I did there?)—because surrender comes with the recognition that you are unable to save yourself. In the context of faith, surrender is an admission of the sovereignty of a greater authority. An admission of your dependence on a greater power. And—this is big—it's an admission that you're willing to place yourself under that authority and power because you know it is absolutely the best, most loving place you could possibly be.

Surrender is what we see in the first couple of bars of an old hymn: "Take my life, and let it be, consecrated, Lord, for Thee."

Simply acknowledging God will not save us, my friends.

James 2:19 addresses the human tendency to believe and then go no further in our relationship with the Lord. James wrote, "You believe that God is one. Good! Even the demons believe—and they shudder!" It's fine and well and good to believe that there is one God, but so do demons. If we stop at just belief or acknowledgment, then we're missing the saving grace that accompanies surrender to Jesus.

Look at Matthew Henry's take:

> But to . . . take up a good opinion of thyself, or of thy state towards God, merely on account of thy believing in him, this will render thee miserable. . . . To rehearse that article of our creed, therefore, I believe in God the Father Almighty, will not distinguish us from devils at last, unless we now give up ourselves to God as the gospel directs, and love him, and delight ourselves in him, and serve him.[5]

Don't settle for just acknowledging God. There is such joy that comes from trusting Him for salvation, living for Him, loving Him, and following wherever He leads.

Surrender to the One who is your all in all.

READ JAMES 2:18–26.

1. Have you ever felt content to go through the motions with your faith? Maybe assumed that you and God were good just because you believe He exists? Or have you seen that assumption play out with a close friend or family member?

2. What does it mean to live a surrendered life?

5. "Commentary on James 2 by Matthew Henry," *Blue Letter Bible*, accessed March 10, 2017, https://www.blueletterbible.org/Comm/mhc/Jam/Jam_002.cfm?a=1148019.

3. Why is it sometimes easier to acknowledge God and stop there? Why is surrender so difficult for us at times?

_____

_____

_____

4. Look up the lyrics to the hymn "Take My Life and Let It Be," and read through them. Write down the verse that most resonates with you.

_____

_____

_____

Today's Prayer

_____

_____

_____

_____

_____

_____

_____

_____

_____

_____

_____

_____

Day 91

$\mathcal{O}$ne of the things I love about my job is that I spend most of my day talking to teenagers. Sometimes those conversations are scheduled, sometimes they're spontaneous, and they're almost always enlightening. I'm not a counselor, so I'm not trying to dig into anyone's life or solve their problems—I'm really just there to listen and "mama" and pray—but I'm consistently surprised by how much information someone can pack into a fifteen-minute, impromptu chat.

There are, of course, a few topics that come up over and over. College. Stress. Friendships. Clothes. Dating. Drama. And it seems like whenever that last topic comes up, another topic quickly follows: social media.

OH, Y'ALL. Social media. As a general rule I really do enjoy it so much, but sometimes, when I see how it affects people I care about, I sort of want to set it on fire.

I know. It's kind of a strong reaction. I'm working on that.

Last week I was thinking about some of the ongoing challenges when it comes to watching teenagers—teenage girls, in particular—navigate the ever-growing social media landscape, and I narrowed my primary concerns down to three. I'm going to keep the explanations short because I had an even bigger epiphany after these three thoughts came to mind.

1. **People sometimes use it as a weapon.** Some people use social media to "rally the troops" against someone who's at the center of drama. Or they leave sarcastic comments and then try to play off what they've said as "just a joke." In other words, people get super childish, but what they forget is that their immaturity can be super hurtful.

2. **People often see what's posted and feel left out.** I totally get that everybody can't be included in every activity. But so many times people will use social media to show what their "friend group" is doing, and when someone hasn't been invited to

participate—or when someone has been lied to about the fact that "nothing is going on tonight"—those pictures can sting.

3. **People can feel pressure to compromise who they are in Christ.** Social media makes people braver than they'd be in real life. People type things they wouldn't normally say, use language they wouldn't normally use, and share pictures they wouldn't necessarily send to their grandmother. All of these things can result in regret, drama, shame, or some combination of the three.

And here's my big epiphany:
Social media is not a requirement in your life.

It is not one of your core courses. It is not a necessary component of fulfilling, rewarding relationships. IT IS OPTIONAL. So if you've hurt people with it, or if you've been hurt by it, or if you've been unwise with your use of it, remember this: you can delete the apps from your phone. You can take a break. You can remove yourself from that particular conversation.

You just might hear the Lord more loudly—and more clearly—than ever.

READ 1 CORINTHIANS 10:23–24.

1. Are you active on social media? Do you follow it dutifully? Just glance at it every once in a while? Not plugged in at all? Has that been a conscious decision or just a by-product of your personality?

_____

_____

2. If your phone were to suddenly disappear, would it change your life at all? Would you miss it?

_____

_____

3. Have you ever fasted from social media? Ever thought about it?

_____

_____

_____

4. Would your friendships be affected if you were to take a break from social media? Explain.

_____

_____

_____

_____

Today's Prayer

_____

_____

_____

_____

_____

_____

_____

_____

_____

_____

_____

_____

_____

Day 92

Y'all might not be able to appreciate this since you've grown up in such a vastly different media environment, but when I was a little kid, my family and I had three TV channels: NBC, CBS, and PBS (we didn't get ABC until cable came on the scene the summer before sixth grade). We had a subscription to the local newspaper, we listened to local radio stations, and if we wanted to watch the news, we'd better be in front of the TV at 5:30 in the afternoon when Walter Cronkite anchored the *CBS Evening News*. Those were our choices. That's it. There weren't any 24-hour news channels, and there was no Internet.

(I know. It was almost like we lived in caves.)

Almost four decades have passed since I was a kid, and needless to say, the media side of things is a whole different deal. Choices are endless, but the irony is that we're constantly narrowing down those options to suit our own preferences. We can customize *everything* these days; we can pick what goes into our news feed, we can choose between who-knows-how-many networks for our news, we can choose newspapers and magazines and websites that align nicely with our political and social views. We can listen to radio stations that only play certain types of music. We can choose from thousands of available TV shows ON OUR PHONES, a reality that would have made my five-year-old brain EXPLODE IN WONDER back in the '70s.

All that to say: *the future is now, y'all.*

But there's something else about our Make-Your-Own media experience that we need to keep in mind: If we're not careful, we can back ourselves into a societal corner where we only listen to, watch, read, and learn from people who see the world though the same lens that we do. And when that's the case, we are missing the blessing, the maturing, and the spiritual stretching that result from being exposed to different ideas and perspectives. Obviously it's great to be secure in your beliefs, but instead of looking for opportunities to spread the gospel, we can grow far too content with preaching to ourselves, with nodding like crazy and amening while we pat each other on the backs for viewing the world the exact same way.

And when people don't agree with us? Well, we can be quick to decide that they're our enemies.

The power of the gospel of Jesus Christ is that it binds what's broken and heals the deepest wounds. It's a bridge that enables us to minister to and with people who are outside the sphere of our daily lives, and that bridge has the power to cross all divides and disagreements. We should absolutely cling to what Scripture tells us is true. But if we don't value the backgrounds and the perspectives of people who live and believe differently than we do, then we're essentially saying we're fine with our respective corners—thanks all the same—because really, what matters most to us is our comfort, our point of view, and our agenda.

For what it's worth, I think we're better than that. Not to mention that Jesus demands more.

The gospel is not an island. It's not a gate. It's not a wall. Let's be willing to set aside our personal preferences, move out of our comfortable corners, and build some bridges in Jesus' name.

READ 1 CORINTHIANS 9:16–23.

1. How is your life programmed to suit your preferences? Think about it for a few minutes, and then explain.

2. Where are you most likely to run into opinions that are different from your own? School? Church? Social media? Traditional media? Friends?

3. Would you say that, generally, you live within sort of a comfort zone? Or are you regularly confronted with situations that challenge your comfort?

_____

_____

_____

4. Do you ever think about how the gospel can make a difference right where you live? Is that something you've experienced?

_____

_____

_____

Today's Prayer

_____

_____

_____

_____

_____

_____

_____

_____

_____

_____

_____

Day 93

Really, if you think about it, we have such a short amount of time here on earth.

Sometimes it feels like you have forever—like the years are creeping by. But the older you get, the more you start to realize that this life is lightning fast. And when you begin to appreciate how quickly the days move from high school to college to career to, you know, retirement (with all sorts of great stuff in between, of course), you can't help but examine how you're living your life. Are you making the most of your time here? Are you investing in other people? Are you living on purpose for the kingdom?

It's not uncommon that, when we ask ourselves those questions, our focus can get all wonky (and yes, that is an official scientific term). We start to put all sorts of burdens on ourselves to "get it right"—feeling the pressure to perform and do better and quit wasting time—and when that happens, we're inevitably confronted with (and reminded of) our sinfulness, our shortcomings, and our failures. And before we even realize it, we've taken ourselves out of the game, so to speak. We think and act like God can't possibly know how to handle our weaknesses.

- We wonder if God is really for us.
- We think His mercy has limits.
- We assume His grace stops right before it reaches us.
- We decide that our sins are unforgiveable.
- We worry that we're not enough.
- We clutter our thoughts with worst-case scenarios.
- We cower at the first hint of fear.
- We dismiss the unique ways the Lord has gifted and called us.
- We doubt His power to redeem our sin, our brokenness, and our failures.
- We question His ways.
- We depend on ourselves instead of Him.

What a relief to know *we* are not the source of ultimate power, and we are not the point. What a relief to know we serve a God whose grace is sufficient and whose strength is made perfect in our weakness (2 Corinthians 12:9). What a relief to know He has created us, He has appointed our time on this earth, and He holds the plan for all our days. What a relief to know that when we surrender our lives to Him, He will give us everything we need to make the most of our time on earth.

- Our heavenly Father pursues us.
- He knows everything about us.
- He loves us unconditionally.
- He provides for us.
- He never forgets or forsakes us.
- He makes a way for us.
- He comforts us.
- He restores us.
- He heals us.
- He saves us and sets us free.
- He leads us and sustains us moment by moment by moment.

There's no doubt that all of our time on our earth is precious. It is fleeting. It is fast. But we serve an unchanging, eternal God who holds all our days in the palm of His hand. When we live with deep dependence on Him (not ourselves!) and unwavering trust in Him (not ourselves!), we live on purpose. We walk by faith, not by sight (2 Corinthians 5:7). And we won't miss what matters most.

READ PSALM 103:15–22.

1. When you think back on, say, first grade, does it feel like yesterday or does it seem like forever ago?

2. Do the years seem to move faster as you get older?

_____

_____

3. Do you ever wonder if you're doing enough with the life you've been given?

_____

_____

4. What do you believe is the biggest purpose of your time here on earth? If you're not sure, jot down a few thoughts that pop into your mind.

_____

_____

Today's Prayer

_____

_____

_____

_____

_____

_____

_____

_____

_____

_____

_____

_____

Day 94

So there's a day coming—or maybe it's already come—when you take everything you've learned from your parents and teachers and youth leaders and pastors, and you somehow have to put all that stuff into practice in the real world.

In big ways and small ways, you have to figure out who you are when no one is looking. You have to figure out how your faith informs and affects your everyday life. You have to figure out how you're going to handle your finances. You have to figure out how you're going to establish boundaries in your dating life. You have to figure out how you're going to show responsibility and integrity in your college life, in your work life, in your personal life.

I know. It's a lot, isn't it? And for the most part, there won't be anybody looking over your shoulder. In fact, a few weeks ago I was talking to a friend who's in college, and she said, "It's so weird how there's nobody reminding me to spend time with the Lord. There's not really anybody who's concerned about my spiritual life. And it feels strange, honestly, after the bubble of high school."

In some respects, this is exactly why your late teens and early twenties can be some of the most exciting days of your life. Yes, there are hard lessons and harsh realities. No doubt. But, Lord willing, it's when you'll really get the hang of putting feet to your faith, when you'll take a whole new level of ownership in terms of immersing yourself in Christian community and building relationships that offer loving accountability. Hopefully it's when nothing and no one can stop you from chasing after the Lord, from pursuing His very best in every aspect of your life.

But can I tell you something in the interest of being completely candid?

No matter how noble and pure your intentions are, you're gonna mess up.

And it's gonna be okay.

And then you're gonna mess up again.

And it's still gonna be okay.

It would be oh-so-awesome if we could just *make up our minds* to grow up and grow into our faith. But much like a kid who's figuring out how to make the transition to riding a bike without training wheels, you're going to fall down sometimes. You're going to get hurt. You might even wind up with a few bruises. And it's in these moments of trial and error, of falling and failure, when God's grace will meet you. It will help you, it will pick you up, and it will sustain you.

Every time grace picks you up—every time you recommit your life and your heart to God's will and His purposes—that same grace that holds you will teach you. It will remind you over and over again that you belong to Jesus, and no matter what kind of learning curve awaits you as you launch into the next phase of your life, and no matter how hard the climb is, it won't be too steep for Him. He'll lead you every step of the way.

READ COLOSSIANS 1:3–14.

1. Do you feel like you've experienced moments when you've had to examine how your faith "operates," so to speak, when you're away from your normal environment?

2. As a general rule, what's your attitude about growing up and getting older? Are you excited? Hesitant? Scared? A combination of all three?

3. In our current culture, do you think the late teens and early twenties are viewed as a time to dig deep into faith? Or do you think the norm is to see that time of life almost like a "free pass" from faith?

4. What potential consequences do you think could result from the "free pass" mentality? Explain.

Today's Prayer

Day 95

*E*arlier tonight I found myself on an Internet rabbit trail. You know how it goes: you look up something, and then you click on something else, and that reminds you of something else, and before you know it you are watching the 2014 Mississippi State versus Auburn football game because you were there with your sister and Mississippi State won the game and went on to be ranked #1 in the country and that particular Saturday was one of the BEST DAYS IN THE HISTORY OF EVER.

That's a purely hypothetical situation, of course. Except for the fact that every single bit of it is true.

Tonight's unexpected trip down football memory lane brought so many details about that day to mind: how Sister and I stood in the blazing sun and waited for Dawg Walk, how the umbrella she had tucked in her purse saved us from certain pre-Dawg Walk heat stroke, how we tailgated with my friend Daphne and her family, how Sister got soaked during a second-quarter downpour thanks to the stadium's no-open-umbrella policy, and how we stayed in the stadium for a solid hour after the game because we couldn't bear to leave the celebration. In so many ways and for so many reasons, it was an epic afternoon.

And tonight, as I watched and remembered, I realized that there was a little kernel of resignation wiggling around in the back of my mind: *That was as good as it gets. There will never be a game as fun as that one.*

What is that, y'all? Why are we prone to think that our best, most memorable days are behind us? Why do we sometimes look toward the future with one foot in the past and our hands covering our eyes?

I mean, I'm just as sorry as I can be about bombarding you with a bunch of rhetorical questions, but I think that's a real thing we do. We get nostalgic about the past—or even the present—and we decide that it's impossible for the future to be as good, much less better. Sometimes we'd even prefer to live in the past, constantly recounting memories, rather than anticipating what's ahead.

But, oh, do I ever have some good news for us. *When we are followers of Jesus Christ, our best days are always ahead.* Always. That's because no matter what—even when there are tough circumstances in front of us—the Lord is always in the business of miraculous, sanctifying works of mercy and grace in our lives. He is always working out a new and better thing. He is always refining us, shaping us, changing us, and preparing us not just for our futures this side of heaven, but also for the kingdom to come.

"Remember whens" can be oh-so-enticing. After all, I spent almost an hour reliving a football game from several years ago. And although it's almost always encouraging to remember the Lord's faithfulness in our pasts, it's also a true gift of grace to be able to confidently look to the future and know that the Lord has already prepared a way for us. He has already made something beautiful. We just have to walk into it, trusting Him, resting in the assurance that whatever lies ahead will be *even better* than what we leave behind.

READ ISAIAH 35:1-10.

1. To some extent, at least, do you tend to idealize the past? Do you romanticize the way things used to be or maybe even feel sad that you can't go back to the way things were?

_____

_____

_____

2. What is one life event that you would absolutely, one hundred percent relive if you could? What was so special about it? Explain.

_____

_____

_____

3. Do you ever wish you could freeze time and keep things exactly as they are?

4. How do you generally view the future? With excitement? With a little trepidation? Does it ever make you fearful?

Today's Prayer

*O*ne day last week, my son and I were talking about books, and I offhandedly mentioned that I missed teaching English because I used to love reading *To Kill a Mockingbird* with my students. "It was my *favorite*," I said. "Sometimes it makes me sad that I don't get to do that anymore."

Alex was quiet for a few seconds, and then he piped up with a question: "So Mama, does that mean you don't like your new job?"

That's not what I said at all, of course. My new(-er) job is all manner of fun. But I understood that Alex heard my words and then arrived at a conclusion: *if I miss what I used to do, then I must not be happy in what I'm currently doing.*

I assured him I love the job I have now, and then I said this: "Just because God calls you to something new doesn't mean you won't miss the old thing."

Oh, y'all. It's *so* important that we get that.

And if we have any questions about whether or not that's normal or biblical or whatever, we need only look at the apostle Paul.

I mean, you probably know this already, but Paul moved around a lot. He would minister in one area, and when God would call him to the next place, he'd get up and go. But we see over and over in his letters that he missed the people and places he'd left behind. He was invested in them and cared deeply for them, but he valued obedience more than his relational or personal comfort.

The older you get, the more you'll find yourself—like Paul—immersed in transition. You'll move to a different city, you'll buy a house in a new neighborhood, you'll change jobs, you'll meet new people, you'll join a different church, and you'll serve in foreign countries. Lord willing, you'll do all of those things under the covering and counsel of the Holy Spirit. And each time the Lord calls you to something new, you'll have two specific opportunities:

1. To leave the old thing with deep gratitude for what the Lord taught you and how He changed you through those people and that place.
2. To walk into the new thing with your heart and your arms wide open, ready for a new adventure with the Lord and the people waiting there for you.

At some point you're going to miss people or place or position. It's a natural reaction to change. After all, we can't compartmentalize the Christian life, so we don't finish one phase of our lives, put it on a shelf, and walk away from it forever. We're constantly learning, constantly synthesizing, and constantly marveling at the amazing tapestry God weaves together. He is always—*always*—at work in our circumstances as He shapes us into the person He's calling us to be. It won't always be easy.

But from that perspective, we can look at the past with fondness, knowing that through it the Lord was teaching us what we needed for the here and now. And for reasons we can't yet know or see, the present will be just as worthwhile.

READ 1 THESSALONIANS 2:1–12.

1. Is there something from your past that you miss? Maybe it's an old house, or your former church, or a certain year of school that was all sorts of awesome? Think about it, and list more than one thing if you'd like.

_____

_____

_____

_____

2. Think about this current season of your life. What do you think you'll miss about it as you get older and move (literally and figuratively) away from it? What's been special about it?

_____

_____

3. Can you look at your past and see specific ways God prepared you for your current stage of life? Explain.

_____

_____

4. Look up Philippians 1:8. Write, doodle, or illustrate it here.

_____

_____

Today's Prayer

_____

_____

_____

_____

_____

_____

_____

_____

_____

_____

_____

Day 97

This afternoon I went to the wedding of a former student. We met when she was in eleventh grade, and I have adored her ever since. A few weeks ago, in fact, I went to one of her bridal showers. And as we all sat in a circle and watched her unwrap her wedding gifts, I thought about how much care and compassion I've seen this particular bride offer people over the years. She loves the Lord, loves to minister, loves to serve. She and her new husband are absolutely perfect for each other, and I am so excited to see what the Lord is going to do through the ministry of their marriage.

So many times, I think, people sort of expect that this is how life will go: they'll finish high school, finish college, get married, and then grown-up life will officially begin. That may very well be the case. But more than likely there will be some variables in that equation. You might decide you don't want to finish college. You might decide to keep going after college and earn two more degrees. You might not get married for ten or fifteen years after you complete your education. Or you might not get married at all.

It's interesting, though, that for many people, marriage is a part of God's plan where they would really like to have some say-so. They would like to determine that, *Yes, this is going to happen for me by such-and-such age.* Or *No thanks, God—because if it's all the same to you, I can live really happily without having to meet someone else's needs; I can barely take care of myself.* And listen, I totally understand both mentalities. It's so easy to get fixated on a time line, to be ready to fall in love (or not) and get married (or not) and get on with whatever's next.

But marriage may or may not be part of God's plan for your life. And as much as you might like to know what God has in store in terms of your future relationships, you're not going to know that, say, tomorrow. You're not going to get a note from the Lord that says, *"Dear Beloved Child, here's what I've decided is best for you regarding marriage."* Just like in a thousand other areas of your life, the Lord will reveal His plan when it's time.

What you can control, though, is how you live your life between the now and the then. You can make wise choices. You can commit to serving Him at all ages and stages. Because as much as we might think otherwise, marriage is not the end goal of our lives on earth. Neither is our independence, for that matter.

So remember: there are parts of the future that you just can't plan, and since that's the case, you certainly don't have to stress about them. The Lord will take care of you no matter what. He knows better than anyone that the primary purpose of your life is to glorify Him, and no matter where He leads, you want to be able to serve and lead without regrets. So wherever you are in your life, dig deep. Seek to know Him more and more. Honor Him in every season of your life.

Enjoy Him, worship Him, and make His name known. His time line is infinitely better than anything we could construct for ourselves.

READ 1 TIMOTHY 4:6–16.

1. Do you ever think about your wedding? Ever wonder what it might be like?

_____

_____

_____

2. Do you think you have an idealistic view of marriage, a realistic view, or a pessimistic view? Explain.

_____

_____

_____

3. Do you ever think about the ways that, as a single person, you could have a meaningful, beautiful life that impacts others for the kingdom of God?

4. Are there any goals you'd like to achieve in your twenties?

Today's Prayer

Day 98

I get that this will make me seem like I'm 104 years old (not that there's anything wrong with that), but my husband and I have watched the TV show *Survivor* since its very first season back in 2000. I realize that many of you weren't even born in 2000, so you'll just have to trust me when I tell you that somehow *Survivor* has managed to hold our attention and our interest for sort of an astonishing number of years.

Well. The other day I was catching up on a couple of episodes from the most recent season while I was cooking supper, and one of the contestants was analyzing his state of mind before he started playing the game.

"I've had a gigantic fear of death," he said, "and over the years it's morphed into something far worse: a fear of life." His words stopped me in my tracks. I rewound the DVR so I could hear his statement again, and I thought, *That is it! For so many people, that is it!*

WE FEAR LIFE.

I don't mean that we're scared that life is going to jump out from a dark doorway, but we fear all the ways life asks us to be vulnerable, to stick our necks out, to take chances. We look for our security in our circumstances instead of resting in the security of being loved and known by God.

- Instead of taking a big shot and trying to make a wide-open basket, we do the safer thing and pass the ball.
- Instead of applying to an out-of-state college that we can't stop thinking about, we do the safer thing and register at a nearby school.
- Instead of asking a teacher for feedback on a short story we've written, we do the safer thing and file the story in a computer folder.
- Instead of singing on the worship team at church, we do the safer thing and confine our singing to the pew.

- Instead of starting a Bible study for younger girls, we do the safer thing and tell ourselves that we're not qualified and that they probably wouldn't show up anyway.

In little ways and big ways, we fear life.

And to a certain extent, we fear for good reason. Life is messy and risky. Every day brings a fresh opportunity to embarrass ourselves, fail miserably, and endure some degree of humiliation in front of other people.

But Scripture offers certainty that soothes our fear and our doubt. Scripture says, "The boundary lines have fallen for me in pleasant places; indeed, I have a beautiful inheritance" (Psalm 16:6). Scripture says, "Do not be afraid or discouraged, for the LORD your God is with you wherever you go" (Joshua 1:9). Scripture says, "Don't be afraid, little flock, because your Father delights to give you the kingdom" (Luke 12:32).

So when the Lord leads us—whether it's by gifting us in certain ways or nudging us in certain directions—we don't have to be afraid. He is our Shepherd and our security. Even when the world might say we've failed, we have the peace of knowing that we've been obedient to what God asked of us.

Heads up, everybody. Eyes wide open. Live boldly for the One who created and called you. YOU HAVE NOTHING TO FEAR.

READ PSALM 16:5–11.

1. Do you consider yourself a fearful person?

2. If you had to name one thing you fear more than anything else, what would it be?

3. Would you say that, to a certain extent, you have a fear of living? Maybe not in general but in a specific area or two?

4. Look up Psalm 34:4. Write, doodle, illustrate it here.

Today's Prayer

Day 99

*A*t some point (almost) every day I make a quick scroll through what my mama liked to call "the Facebook." I love to see pictures of my friends' families, I watch the minute-long cooking videos that pop up in my feed, and I check to see who's having a birthday. In a way, Facebook is like being at school and listening to the morning announcements; it's a quick overview of what's happening on any given day.

About a year ago I was in the middle of my daily Facebook scroll, and although I can't remember if I just ran across it or someone recommended it, I saw a video of CeCe Winans singing "Blessed Assurance" at a *Kennedy Center Honors* performance. "Blessed Assurance" is one of the hymns I vividly remember singing when I was a little girl. I don't know that I was terribly impacted by the lyrics, but I loved the cadence and the rhythm of the song.

So. I clicked the "play" button, and the emotion of hearing the first few bars took me by surprise.

Blessed assurance, Jesus is mine!
Oh, what a foretaste of glory divine!
Heir of salvation, purchase of God,
Born of His Spirit, washed in His blood.

I've sung those words hundreds of times in my life, but the truth of them hit me in a completely new way. So if you'll bear with me, I'd like to pass along a little encouragement.

I can't presume to know what's going on in your life right now. Maybe you're in the middle of an idyllic few months where everything seems rosy, and you can barely remember what it's like to feel worried or discontent. Maybe you're on the front end of what looks like a grueling stretch in school or at home or at work. Maybe you're so covered up in apathy right now that you don't even care about what's going on. I can relate to every bit of that.

And I think most of us can get so deep in the business of real life, so wrapped up in seemingly urgent circumstances, that we lose sight of the assurance we have in Jesus. We forget that every single day, in every single situation, He is working in and through our lives to prepare us for eternity with Him. He does that not because of anything we've done, but because of His mercy and grace. He has made us heirs. He has made us His own. His Spirit lives inside us because we trust that the blood of Jesus has covered all our sins.

That being said, it's frustratingly easy to become blasé about what we believe. It's incredibly humbling to realize how often we put our faith in what we can see as opposed to what we can't (2 Corinthians 4:18).

Even still, when we belong to Jesus, the Lord faithfully assures us of our salvation. He assures us in and through Scripture, and by the power of the Holy Spirit, He assures us in the day-to-day. He affirms, He confirms, He blesses, He comforts, and He heals. Over and over again He makes a way for us.

He is our greatest treasure. *He* is our greatest confidence. *He* is our greatest hope.

Blessed assurance, indeed.

READ 1 JOHN 5:6–12.

1. Have you ever been reduced to tears when you've heard someone sing a hymn or a praise song?

_____

_____

2. Is there one in particular that's consistently meaningful or inspirational to you?

_____

_____

3. What are some of the daily stresses or frustrations that sometimes interrupt your "blessed assurance," so to speak?

_____

_____

_____

4. Look up the lyrics to "Blessed Assurance." Write down the last stanza here.

_____

_____

_____

Today's Prayer

_____

_____

_____

_____

_____

_____

_____

_____

_____

_____

_____

_____

Day 100

*O*h, y'all.

My heart is a little tender right now. Honestly, I could cry if I let myself. Because if you're on the last day of this book, that means we've spent one hundred days together. ONE HUNDRED DAYS. It's a significant stretch of time, you know? And I get that it probably sounds strange since most of us have never met in person, but I am really going to miss getting to spend time with you. In that funny way the Lord works, He has somehow connected us through the words on these pages. It has been such an honor to serve you, and I hope that these last one hundred days have been an encouragement. I hope that the Lord has helped you settle some things. I hope that you've grown in your relationship with Him, that you've been reminded of His deep love for you, and that you're secure in the knowledge that there is no greater joy than serving Him with your whole life.

So. As we wrap up our time together (in this book, at least, because I may miss you so much that I show up at your house one day), it seems right and fitting to close with a letter from my heart to yours. Because although I trust that you'll keep learning and growing and digging deep into a life of faith, I also believe with everything in me that the Lord has kingdom work for you in the here and now. And let me tell you: when I think about you stepping into that—when I think about you loving people really well in Jesus' name—it makes me teary-eyed. I am so proud of you.

All righty. Here we go.

My sister in Christ,

The God who made the whole world also made you.
He designed you with great purpose.
He planned your life so that you would walk the earth at this specific time.
He knows you better than anyone, and He loves you unconditionally.
Your identity is always and only in Him.
He has called you by name, and you are His. (Isaiah 43:1)

He has grafted you into the family of God. (Romans 11:17)
He has given you everything you need for life and godliness. (2 Peter 1:3)
He has equipped you for every good work. (2 Timothy 3:17)

So, as my mama used to say: get out there and get after it.

Love Him with everything you have.
Serve people whenever and however you can.
Follow wherever He leads.
Share the gospel.
Make His name known.

And when the world gets loud, remind yourself:

He is everything.
He is worth everything.
And if He is all you have, you have all you need.

He is your all in all.

> Now to him who is able to do above and beyond
> all that we ask for or think according to the power that
> works in us—to him be glory in the church and in
> Christ Jesus to all generations, forever and ever. Amen.
> —Ephesians 3:20–21

READ PSALM 33.

1. What's one thing the Lord has taught you over the last one hundred days?

_____

_____

_____

2. Moving forward, is there any area where you feel especially challenged in your relationship with the Lord?

_____

_____

3. Is there any area—friends, school, service—where you're convicted to live or serve differently?

_____

_____

4. Way back in the introduction of the book, I mentioned Colossians 1:15–20. Look up that passage and read it out loud. (Trust me—it's *strong*.)

_____

_____

Today's Prayer

_____

_____

_____

_____

_____

_____

_____

_____

_____

_____